MW00627156

THE BREAKING POINT

Melanie,

Thank you for your support!

Sondra King

THE BREAKING POINT

POINT

When Life Requires a Shift

PAULETTE HARPER

Thy Word Publishing
California

Published by Thy Word Publishing

Antioch, CA 94531

© 2022 Paulette Harper

Book Cover Design: Tyora Moody
Interior Book Design & Formatting: https://tywebbincreations.com
Editor: Paulette Nunlee https://fivestarproofing.com

All rights reserved. No part of this book may be used or reproduced, stored in or introduced into a retrieval system, or transmitted in any form including, photocopying, electronic or mechanical, recording or by any means without the express written consent from the author.

Scripture quotations marked "NKJV" are taken from the New King James Version. Copyright © 1982 by Thomas Nelson, Inc. Used by permission. All rights reserved.

Scripture quotations marked "KJV" are taken from the Holy Bible, King James Version, Cambridge, 1769. Used by permission.

Library of Congress Cataloging-in-Publication Data

Paperback: ISBN- 978-1-7370931-4-5

E-book: 978-1-7370931-3-8

Published and printed in the United States of America.

FOUNDING SUPPORTERS

Amanda Ducksworth

Akaasha Ziya

Andre Swinney

Adah Mcrae

Alice Gaskins

Angelique Bullock

Arlisia Hughes

Annie M. Kelley

AriDigs

Angela Bennett

Ann Carethers

Acy Brown

Alex Morton

Andrea Harmon

Ashley Smith

Alisa Goode

Ann Boehm

Anthony Whitaker

Awetsh Kassa

Angelia Steward

Beverly Owens

Beverly Starks

Brwnskn Yoga

Brianna Bryant

Barbara Carter

Brownie Sims

Brendalyn Young

Brittney Barlow-Becton

Beverly Frank

Brenda Thompson

Brenda & Nichole

Byron Bull

Beulah Williams

Cookie Hamilton

Cheryl Latimer

Chastity Moore

Cecilia Harris

Cherry Collins

Chrissy Cummings

Colleen Carter

Carla Jacobs

Cindi Franz

Cynthia Crutchfield

Cameshia Payne

Christina Tofaeono

Cristine Hillman

Cherri Rushing

Christolenae Thomas

Cynthia Franklin

Carla Keith

Carmen Woods

Chiffon Graves

Dr.Sharlene Waldron-Kinlock

Daequan Kirkland Sr

Danielle Busby

Daryl Humdy

Damon Owens

Debbie Magee

Dana Anderson

Debbie Howard

Deloris Vaughn

Dollene Howell

Dunia Thornton

Doris Hamel-Humdy

DAM Sport Fitness

Darnell & Renee Mack

David Diouf

Deborah Preston

David Goberdhan

Desire Maison

Donise Lei

Dr. Jessica David

Dennis and Tenisha Williams

Dr. Lonnie Morris

Dr Linda Washington

Dr Vincent Manyweather

Dr. Yolanda Jerry YJ Empowerment Solutions

Deborah Walker

Doug Rogers

Dena Richard

Daniel Crockett

Erika R Jones

Elizabeth Williams

Elizabeth Anderson

Elizabeth Hutson

Emmett Mapp

Ezreaonne Jackson

Edmen McNary

Erica Mosby

Estella Warner

Erin Malloy Home Baked Sweet-
ness by E

Elizabeth Hunter

First Lady Jewel Parris

Fanny Roberson

Fannie Hill

Gary Shumlai

Geneva Hopkins

Glenda Yarbrough

Geneva Hopkins

Geneva Swift Hopkins

Genene Hopkins

Hartte Marbury

Hattie Bivens

Ilia Steward

Ida Dorsey

Joyce Mangium

Joe Arnold

Jonathan Lawshe

James and Eugenia Johnson

Janice Prasad-Humdy

J. D. Kelley

Janice Jones

Joyce Underwood

Jacalyn Evone Robinson

Jasmine Harris

Joey Bumpus

Joanne Rogers

Juliana Taylor

Joanne Johnson-Cobbs

Katrina Carter

Kartriece Ward

Kat Roux CEO of Eternally Lit Smiles

Kingston Morton

Karen Rampersaud

Kimberly Hall

Kyanna Beard

Katrina Moore

Konica McMullen

Kimberly Merritt

Kiayana Sydnor

Kaijah Dawson

Kim Jacobs of The Kim Jacobs Show

Karen Murray

Katherine Gaines

Kelsi Arceneaux

Kenya Taylor

Kenny Lane

Latoria Powell

Linda Carter Player

LaSaundra Owens

Latonya Pye

Lashonda Johnson Gibson

Lydia Abel

Lamonte Gray Jr.

LaTosha Holliman

Lillie Hopkins

Lee Griffin

Leonor Gonzalez, All City Notary

Mary Ward Allen

Merry D. Anderson

Mrs. Michael Hunter

Mary A Graham

Michelle Dundas

Morales Lewis

Monique Washington

Mable Coburn

Melanie Little

Melody Payne

Michele Lynette

Millie Hopkins

Monica Gray

Mariama Smith-Parker

Matt Desouza

Marvin Jones

Marie Murray

Melissa Wellman

MelRose B. Corley

Monique Denton-Davis

Marquitta Dixon

Margrett Rose

Marilyn Locke

Michelle L Stephens

Monica Jones

Melonie Renee Hudson

Myndi Baker LSW

Melinda McLemore

Malachi Harrell

Marvin Harrell

Mary Martin

Monique Gunter

Ngozi Asonye

Nelijah Carminer

Nia Bryant

Nicolette Bryant

Natasha Sawyer

Nicole Eason

Paris Rathel

Patricia Swift Peete

Patricia Ferrell

Patrice Mothie

Pastor Nadine Grigsby

Pastor Vestina Oates

Pastor Vivian Ijeoma

Paul McRae

Pauline Evans

Puah Neiel

Patricia Melton

Pascha Clay

Qheem Edmonds

Rodney Johnson

Renaldo Harte

Rogina Vaughn

Raquel Cummings

Rev. Adunnola Waterman-French

Rev. Paul Heyliger

Rebecca Grice

Renshel Franklin

Ronald Bennett

Rosa Lee Bennett

Rosalind Black

Rodney Pontiflet

Rosalind Jswata

Raymond Powell

Raymond Cooper

Richey Martin

THE BREAKING POINT

Sharee Johnson

Sharon Johnson

Sheena Kelley

Shelita Davis

Sherrenique Jones

Sandra Gray

Sandra Harte

Sandra Pompey

Sandriena Joseph

Seon Clarke

Shondel Jackson-Wills

Stephen Akwaeke

Sabrina Smith

Susan Obmoin

Shaina Aldridge

Stephen Starks

Sybil Hopkins

Shurvone Wright

Sabrina Abercrombie

Shonda Christmas

Stacy Henderson

Sarah Swearingin

Sophia Hayes-Jackson

Shannon Curtis Realtor

The Lighthouse of Prayer

Tracie P Tucker

Tony Beard

Trudy Hunter

Tamakin Fox

Tauris Nelson

Thelma Beard

Tiffany Swift

Toni Jones

Trudy Hunter

True Believers

Tina Marquez

Tyrone Powell

Terri Levels

Terrial Davenport

Toni Rollins

Victoria Locklyn

Vanessa Wyche

Valerie Edwards

Veronica Edwards

Vanessa Busby

VerRon Busby

PAULETTE HARPER

Wendy StoltzSond

William Collier

Watisha Ward

Yvonne Smith

Yolanda K Churchwell

Zenny Oluwo

INTRODUCTION

Paulette Harper

A MESSAGE FROM THE VISIONARY AUTHOR

PASTOR PAULETTE HARPER

Twelve Times Best-Selling Author | Empowerment
Speaker | Ordained Pastor | Certified Story Coach

The *Breaking Point* is my fifth book collaboration. When
I set out on this journey, I had not envisioned coaching
over one hundred men and women to become authors.

When God called me to write, He placed a passion in my
heart to help others fulfill their own dreams of sharing
their stories with the world and taking center stage as
they shine in a world that desperately needs their words
that empower and inspire. The *Breaking Point* is such a
book.

These twenty women and men, some first-time authors,
said *yes* to the transformation; *yes* to the stretching; *yes* to

going back to those dark places that brought them pain. Because they knew what they experienced wasn't just for them, but it was for others who will come behind them needing those words to pull them up and help them move to a place of wholeness. These authors are writing from a place of victory, a place where they are no longer the victim.

The Breaking Point is stories by men and women on how they came to that turning point and were able to overcome adversity and reach their own personal breakthrough in life.

Each story will encompass their unique struggle of how they overcame the challenges to find that you had the courage, the power, and the resolve to build your life again.

This book will serve as a potent reminder that everyone has the power to choose which direction they want for their own lives.

Are you ready to take the journey with us? Buckle your seatbelt. Your life will never be the same.

The Breaking Point... when life requires a shift!

Your Visionary Author,
Paulette Harper
www.pauletteharper.com

ABOUT THE AUTHOR

Paulette Harper is a speaker, certified creativity coach, business coach and global voice for emotional wellness and personal development. She teaches women how to change the narrative and turn those painful experiences into writing best-selling books, starting businesses and creating programs.

She specializes in helping women shift their perspective on crises, push past barriers and discover their purpose, so they become the best version of themselves.

As an author of Christian Fiction, nonfiction and children's books, she has over eleven literary works to her credit. Two-time award winning author Paulette Harper's fictional debut *Secret Places Revealed* won national acclaim by becoming the Emma Award Winner for Inspirational and Spiritual Romance.

In addition, her nonfiction book *Completely Whole* achieved national recognition by winning the Readers Favorite Award for best Christian Non-Fiction.

She has been featured on ABC, CBS, NBC and the Sacramento Observer.

Connect with Paulette

- Website: www.pauletteharper.com
- Facebook: https://www.facebook.com/profile.php?id=100010047302425
- Link tree: https://linktr.ee/pauletteharper

LOVE BROKE ME

Betty Collier

"We have not come into the world to be numbered; we have been created for a purpose; for great things; to love and be loved."

~ Mother Teresa

Can loving and being loved actually cause a breaking point? I pondered that for quite some time as I contemplated what I deemed my undeserving place in this book. I wondered if I had truly experienced something so monumental that my life required a shocking reboot? It was only after I prayed about it that my answer was an outrageously loud affirmative. While it may not be the horrific or cataclysmic ordeal others have fought for dear life to overcome, you may be able to relate to my much more subtle, but no less powerful breaking point which catapulted my life's trajectory into places I never imagined.

My first breaking point actually occurred a week before high school graduation in the aftermath of a physical assault by a classmate. That near-death experience began with a skull fracture and ended with emergency surgery to remove an epidural hematoma (blood clot) on the brain of an eighteen-year-old.

That eighteen-year-old was William Collier. He was and still is the absolute love of my life. He is also my beloved husband of thirty-five years and counting. In my heart, I truly believe God saved his life back in May, 1983 because he was created just for me. He's part of my story, and had he not gone through such a horrendous nightmare, we probably never would have gotten married. We fell in love as fourteen-year-olds in ninth grade. We also broke up in high school and would have gone our separate ways after graduation had God not allowed that dreadful misfortune to take place.

"I hope that boy don't die."

Those were the inadvertent words my mother spoke when she first heard the news about William's assault that sent me spiraling out of control. We had grown so far apart that I didn't even know what happened to him a week before our high school graduation. He was clinging to life when he was taken to the second emergency room after the first one (unknowingly) sent him home to die with an undiagnosed medical emergency. The blood clot was so severe that the brain surgeon was quite certain it would have killed him if he had not rushed him into the operating room to relieve the tremendous pressure building up on his brain.

Prior to that horrendous calamity, I didn't think I loved him anymore even though he never stopped loving me in high school. However, the thought of losing him shattered my heart into a thousand little pieces. As I reflect on that awful period of our lives, I realize it was only by God's grace and mercy that we were reunited on William's "near-death" bed. I loved that eighteen-year-old boy more than I ever thought possible. Past disappointments and hurt feelings had to be put aside in order to receive the magnificent gift of his beautiful love for me. In turn, I could shower him with that same love.

Just as Mother Teresa said, we were created for a purpose, to love and be loved. The basic definition of love according to Merriam Webster is *strong affection for another arising out of kinship or personal ties; attraction based on sexual desire; affection and tenderness felt by lovers; affection based on admiration, benevolence, or common interests.* While it seems humanly impossible to actually define what love is, there is one thing I know for sure. There is no greater gift than love.

If we never open our hearts and allow love to prevail, we would miss out on so many wonderful things in life.

William and I were on the brink of giving up on each other when love essentially broke us all the way down to a place where eighteen-year-olds rarely go. We spent the two weeks he was in the hospital recovering after emergency surgery getting to know each other all over again while reflecting on what went wrong with our relationship in high school. I never expected to open my heart so wide and let him in, but I did . . . right there in his hospital room where he actually had to get out of his "sick bed" to comfort me as my tears flowed.

JUNE 4, 1983

I remember that day and the look on William's face very well. He was recovering at home by then. It was the day my eighteen-year-old self told William "I LOVE YOU!" I knew when I said it *that* time that it was forever. I had said it before as far back as when I was fourteen. This time though, this time I knew deep on the inside that God had filled my heart with a love for William that would never die.

As insignificant as that may seem, whether you consciously choose to fall in love or it happens without you even realizing it, the main thing to realize is that it is indeed life's greatest gift. Loving and being loved sometimes requires overcoming a vast array of feelings to get to the point that you allow yourself to feel that way and trust the love being given in return.

While the world may debate whether true love exists, I encourage you to open your heart and expect it instead of doubt it. I simply cannot imagine my life without love, without William, without our children, and without the family that we have been blessed to share together. There is an idiom that says "And they lived happily ever after." By definition, an idiom is just an expression, a figure of speech. Love is not a fairy tale; but if you open your mind to the idea of happily living in love, you may just find yourself there.

Although I don't have a dramatic story of how I nursed him back to health once he was discharged from the hospital, I must admit that I smiled every time I heard his father proclaim that I brought William back to life! We were only eighteen, so of course we certainly didn't have all the answers and would have been quite naïve to think otherwise. However, not only did we trust each other, but we also trusted our love for each other. It was something we cherished back then and learned to never take for granted.

Do I wish everyone could marry their high school sweetheart and live happily ever after? Of course! I know that is not realistic though.

Can I give you advice or simple steps to follow to ensure you have a long, successful marriage? Of course not! That's not realistic either.

But what I can do is encourage you to follow your heart. There is no magic formula for meeting the right person or finding the perfect match. We are all imperfect, and what works for one person or couple may not work for the other. William and I grew more in love as time went on. Sure, we had trials and tribulations along the way, but marriage means trusting each other through the good and bad because it is worth it. Communication and honesty are vital components in a relationship. If you can't trust someone to hold your heart gently in their hands without breaking it, save your heart for someone else who will take incredibly good care of it.

I know people long for finding true love. We were blessed to find it while still in our teens. When I thought about my life without William in it, I knew that no matter what it took, I would love him through whatever may come our way. How could I not love this person that I truly believe God made just for me? I couldn't reject my love for him or his love for me.

"Love is when the other person's happiness is more important than your own." —H. Jackson Brown, Jr.

That may very well be the best definition of love that I've

ever heard. It may sound cliché, but think about it. If you put the other person's feelings above your own, and in your heart commit to making that person happy, doesn't that bring you happiness as well? I have discovered the more I try to make William happy and put him first, the happier I am because I love to see him happy.

Let me conclude with this prayer for you:

Dear God,

May those reading this wholeheartedly accept the fact that you created them out of love. Show them that they were created for a great purpose—to love you and each other. Help them to understand your love for them on a deeper and more personal level so that they can learn to share that love with others. Open their hearts to receive natural and supernatural love. Bless them to fully expect to love and be loved.

In Jesus' Name,

Amen

ABOUT THE AUTHOR

Betty Collier has co-authored her second anthology, *The Breaking Point*. She describes herself as a nurse by profession, author by passion, and storyteller by the grace of God. She is the bestselling, award-winning author of the *Living Inside the Testimony* book series, a collection of inspirational nonfiction stories. Betty showcases her gift of storytelling by engulfing her readers from the very beginning and captivating their attention throughout the emotional journeys.

In her second book series, *The Birthday Gift*, Betty displays her storytelling in a surprisingly extraordinary way with her fictional work. She continues to inspire while lifting the words right off the pages to bring her characters to life. Readers will find themselves hoping for the best and dreaming about the characters as if they were members of their own family.

Betty's fictional work is also included in the John 3:16 Global Placement Mission. She uses her creative talent to introduce readers to the greatest gift ever given to mankind. While taking them on intriguing tales of heartbreak and hope, Betty intricately weaves together stories leaving readers in suspense until the very end. What they have in common is they all beautifully deliver the gospel message found in John 3:16.

On a personal note, Betty married the absolute love of her life, William Collier, in 1986 after first meeting him in middle school. They are the proud parents of two sons and a daughter-in-law, all residing in Bartlett, TN.

Connect with Betty

- Facebook.com/BettyCollier.Author
- Twitter.com/BettyCollier
- Instagram.com/bettycollier
- Tiktok.com/@bettycollier1storyteller
- Website: http://livinginsidethetestimony.com
- Email: livinginsidethetestimony@yahoo.com

2

OH BOY

Jane Efua Asamoah

The year 2016 was life changing for me. I welcomed my youngest son, Andrew, in January. I tell you what: That boy came pointing me to Jesus right from infancy! The meaning of the name Andrew is: manly or the mighty one. Andrew in the Bible, Peter's brother, always pointed others to Jesus. And like him, my son arrived pointing his momma to her Savior –Jesus, the Almighty One!

Most believers are very familiar with apostle Peter, but it was apostle Andrew who brought his brother Peter to meet Jesus (John 1:40-42, KJV). It was Andrew who brought the little boy who had the five loaves of bread and two fish to Jesus. (John 6:1-9, KJV). It was Andrew and apostle Philip who brought certain Greeks to Jesus when they came looking for Him (John 12:21-26, KJV).

The significance of Andrew in the Bible and God's use of

my dear Andrew to bring me into a relationship with Him was something I discovered in hindsight two years after his birth. As I was studying the Bible, I made the connection when God reminded me of the story I am about to share.

When I was pregnant with my Andrew, I was praying and hoping for a girl. I even got a pink car seat and collected a suitcase full of girl clothes. So, I was caught off guard when my son made his entrance into the world. Looking back, I think perhaps I developed postpartum depression after his birth, and my dashed hope likely contributed to the lethargy I sank into. I'm not sure if it was because of my disappointment or I was just tired, but I was at a very low point when I left the hospital that lasted for a few months. Thank God I never had suicidal thoughts, but the experience was very stifling.

I lost all motivation to exert myself beyond the minimum amount of energy required of me to take care of my children. I still had my two older boys who were three and six to look after. My normal routine was to drop them off at school and return home to be with my newborn. I would just lie on the couch until it was time to pick up the older boys, only getting up to tend to the needs of my baby. I was going through an unexplainable period of overwhelming sadness. I was dissatisfied with life in general. Clinically, this is known as dysphoria, though I did not know to call it that at the time.

Even in the midst of going through this terrible experience, I still maintained my daily habit of watching Joyce Meyer on television. Her program was the only television I watched, and God used her to help me survive my heavy weight of emotions. Typically, I would turn the television off at the end of Joyce Meyer's program, but for some unknown reason one day *something* said to flip through the channels, which I did. I am so glad I listened to that prompting because God used it to bring me great blessing.

I just happened upon a preacher as he was saying, "Jesus says '*Come unto me, all ye that labor and are heavy laden, and I'll give you rest. (Matthew 11:28 KJV)*' His love does not lie on the 'loveableness' of the one being loved..." That claim grabbed my attention so that I stopped channel-surfing and remained to the end of the program, listening intently. I even ordered the CD recording of the broadcast and listened to it over and over again in the months that followed. I have listened to Pastor Joseph Prince of New Creation Church in Singapore's broadcasts ever since that special day. Through his teachings, I have learned the importance of getting to know God for myself and not depend solely on preachers and teachers for understanding. Right from the start of this journey of personally knowing God, God used Pastor Prince to stir in me a hunger and a thirst to read the Bible and not wait to be spoon-fed by my local church pastor or televangelists.

I took to heart Pastor Prince's admonition to feed on God's Word by getting Bibles for every corner of my house especially right by my water closet. Making the Word easily accessible helped me get started reading the Bible on my own. God also reminded me of Joyce's advice to not hurry through the Bible by means of some goal to read the Bible in a year. She said it was better to take time reading scripture than to hurry through for the sake of a deadline. I remembered her advice to savor the Bible and determined I wasn't going to rush through. I decided to start at the very beginning of the Bible but take my time and let the Holy Spirit set the pace.

So my life in Jesus really began back in that bleak time when I began to read His Word in earnest. I allowed the Holy Spirit freedom to lead and interpret His Word to me. As I read the Bible a desire to know God in a more personal way began to grow in me. I had been in church all my life; but reading His Word made me realize I did not really *know* God at all. I only knew about Him. I wanted to know the Person He is but did not know *how*. I remember praying: "God help me know who You *are*. I want to *know* You." And God was faithful to answer my request.

He introduced Himself to me in a tender and creative way by reminding me of something from my childhood.

When I was eight years old, I wrote an essay in school entitled: "Myself." The assignment was to introduce myself to my class by sharing things that were true about me. Facts like my name, my appearance, my interests, and my pasttimes. God answered my prayer for HOW to go about getting to know Him by bringing to mind that essay. I saw in my memory myself as little girl Jane Efua Harrison standing in front of her class reading her essay about who she was. Just like that, God answered me by saying through that memory I was to use that same guideline of the elementary school assignment for getting to know who He is. Suddenly it was clear how to go about this discovery I longed for. His Holy Spirit explained it to me, like the good teacher He is.

In the essay I first had to introduce myself to the class by telling my name. So in the same manner, God encouraged me to ask Him to introduce Himself to me. He asked me "When you meet someone for the first time, what do you do?" The answer is: Exchange names. And then gradually, if interested in pursuing a relationship with the person, the familiarity progresses from knowing a name to asking other personal things.

Based on that example I understood what God was asking me to ask Him. I began by asking Him His name. I knew His name was "God," but He was inviting me to dig deeper into the Bible and study His many names. I was to begin knowing Him by His name(s). He was inviting me to be curious and explore. And I did! And I still do. It's a lifelong quest full of surprises and wonder, questions and mystery.

This journey began for me a relationship with Him in which I can now say I *know* Him. And I am growing more in love with Him every day. Who He is and what He is like and what He likes and doesn't like becomes clearer and clearer as I listen and ask questions. In this journey I've asked many questions, such as "How old are You, God?" "Where do you live?" "What kind of food do you like to eat?" I have wondered on these questions and others. Answers come through reading a scripture verse, or by way of a television program, a church service, a conversation with my spiritual mom, or during conversation in a small group fellowship and through life experience.

I realize looking back on my story that Andrew had a divine assignment in my life. God knew another boy was what I needed to bring me into a deeper relationship with Him. Even now, when people ask me when I accepted Jesus, or when I began to follow Him, I always have one answer. "When Andrew was born." Because it was in that desperate time that God introduced Himself to me in His tender, personal way. God's Word healed me. Isn't it so much like God to bring good out of evil? Now, I can gladly say that postpartum depression was definitely a blessing in disguise. I wouldn't trade my Andrew for any girl in the world.

ABOUT THE AUTHOR

Jane Efua Asamoah is the author of two children's book; "My Mommy's Name Is Mommy" and "God's Unblinkable Eyes." Her newest book, The Breaking Point, is an adult inspirational book, which she collaborated on with other authors. She enjoys writing in her journal about her unique yet seemingly ordinary encounters with God and people.

She received her Bachelor of Arts degree in sociology from University of Ghana and her master's degree in social work from University of Alabama in Tuscaloosa. She was born and raised in Ghana, West Africa, and has lived most of her adult life in the United States of America.

She sees it as a great joy and honor to partner with other

believers in leading children in the ways of Jesus. Jesus commissioned believers to make disciples and she believes that begins in our homes. Parents can plant the truth of God's Word in their children's minds by reading the Bible with them, living out their own love for God in word and deed and taking them to church where others do the same. But only the Holy Spirit can access the heart and bring about the fruit parents desire to see grow in their children.

A full time mom, she currently lives in Roanoke with her husband and her three precious boys. She serves in her community as a children's supervisor in Bible Study Fellowship.

Her website is www.janeasamoah.com.

3

ALMOST OUT FOR THE COUNT

Melissa Powell

There seemed to be a lot of times when I was almost out for the count and at my breaking point. Breaking point means to me a time when I almost did not make it. A time when I was knocked out and did not think I would make it to the next round or level. A time when it looked like I was defeated and at a point where I would not recover.

Part of my story begins at the beginning in 2005. I suffered a miscarriage on the first day of the year. It was an awful way to start the new year. In pain, I spent my day on the floor of my bathroom. This was my third pregnancy, and I was almost 30 years of age with no children. Having a miscarriage was a painful experience for me. It was physically and emotionally draining. How can this be? Not another miscarriage again? Why, Lord? Why me again,

Lord? Devastated and angry, I was beyond depressed. I could not believe this was happening to me again. I wanted this child so much. I know most people have a lot of goals in life, but I only had two. My deepest desire and only goals were to be a mother and wife. My only two goals seemed so far away. It seemed like a punishment, having been pregnant, and for it only to end in a miscarriage. I was grieving my future. I was grieving my child. I was grieving what could be in my life. It left me hurt, confused, and angry.

I only planned to be a mother and wife, but little did I know that God had other plans for my life. All my other goals and accomplishments were bonuses. I wondered whether I would ever have the joy of being a mother. I wondered whether I could experience what it would be to deliver a healthy baby or have someone call me mom or mother. I can't name the number of baby showers I'd attended and the gifts that I purchased for others who were expecting. I questioned was I destined to be a barren woman. I wanted to be a mother, and I wanted it bad. I thought about Hanna in the Bible and how she prayed for a child, and God answered her prayers. I prayed and prayed some more. I would jokingly say, "Hanna's prayers did not have anything on me" because of the way I prayed for a child. I wanted it and wanted it bad.

Three months later, I found out I was pregnant again. It

22

was not going to be a painless process because I was a dia-
betic. I was newly diagnosed with diabetes, and I did not
know how it would affect my pregnancy. I was on a strict
diet and calorie counting. I was being followed for a high-
risk pregnancy. The medical team did not want me to gain
too much weight too fast. One of the goals was for the
baby not to get too big too fast. Initially, I was able to be
successful in this goal. I lost weight. I was excited about
being pregnant, but I did not want to share it with anyone
until at least four months into the pregnancy. If I reached
four months, I thought I would be safe from a miscarriage.

When I was four months pregnant, I found out that the
person I loved didn't love me, but someone else. I never
will forget the day I found myself on his porch, alone
and pregnant, while the father of my child went into the
house with another woman. It was the death of my dream
and expectations. I was embarrassed, hurt, confused, and
unsure of my next move. My self-esteem was lower than
low. I questioned who I was. Lastly, I asked myself all the
wrong questions. Why was I not enough? Why didn't he
love me? I was going to have his baby. It was the best and
worst time—at the same time. My prayer for a child has
been answered, but I had all this other drama in my life.
My worldview was shattered. My image of us being one
big happy family was gone and not a reality.

I found myself bleeding during the pregnancy—over six

times. The last time, I thought, I had a miscarriage. I was bleeding so bad and didn't want to go to the hospital. I knew the drill; I had been there before. I remembered New Year's Day. Doctors sent me home to let the pregnancy pass. It was painful, and the blood seemed like it would never stop. Sitting on the rug on the floor in my bathroom, I cried over the tub, being physically and emotionally in pain. I didn't want to go through that or even hear the words "It was a spontaneous abortion."

After finding myself at rock bottom, I begged and pleaded with God. I say rock bottom, but it seemed like the bottom had fallen out. I asked God not to let me live this life without being a mother. I did not want to have a miscarriage again.

God answered my request. I never bled or spotted again since that day. I delivered my miracle baby in November. I wish I could say we lived happily ever after, but life taught me some lessons. My biggest lesson is that it is okay to move on and change your status even when the future is unknown. A man will commit to the woman he wants to be with. The right man will love and appreciate me. Know your worth, and don't settle for less. Knowing my worth has been a hard lesson to learn. Some people will never value you if you don't value yourself. They will lowball you or lower your price tag if you allow them to do it. God is our guide, and if we follow Him, we will be okay.

God is a restorer of broken things, including people. I was damaged, broken, and stretched beyond my capacity. I remember someone giving me a book, "Where Is God When It Hurts" by Phillip Yancey. I did not appreciate it at the time. I would later read it and understand that God is with me. This is a lesson that I have cherished and remembered that no matter what I face, God is with me. He is with me in the good times and bad times. He is my rock and strong tower and an ever-present help.

I realized that there are things in life we cannot control. We cannot control the weather, the rainstorms, snowstorms, or showers. We cannot control illness, sickness, or diseases. There were many days I wanted to say, "No God, I don't want this sickness. You should take it back." sometimes we are genetically disposed to diseases because of the family we are born into. I wanted God to take diabetes back. And having a miscarriage was another one. We cannot control death, who dies, why they die or who, when, and why miscarriages happen. We can't control a lot of our circumstances.

Charles R. Swindoll wrote one of my favorite poems, "Attitude" and it says, "The only thing we can control is our attitude and ends with I'm convinced that life is 90% of what happens to me and 10% of how I react to it." It has helped me process situations and realized what I can control and what I can't. I only can change how I respond. It is in Ecclesiastes 3 that states, there is a time for everything, and a season for every activity under the heavens. God has to delay something until we grow up to know He is our source, provider, and He wants to be first in our lives. Life will throw some situations at you that you think you can't manage, but don't let it break you. When times get hard, as they will, keep going. I realized that I could start again. I can bend, but I am not breaking because victory is my destiny. I have learned not to give in or give up when life throws me a curveball or a situation where I almost get knocked out. I made it when I was almost knocked out. I recovered from everything that almost broke and defeated me. Don't settle, but know what you want and get it. When God is with you, you can get up from everything that tried to destroy you.

ABOUT THE AUTHOR

Melissa Harrell is a co-author of *The Breaking Point*.

Melissa is an ordained minister and a devout woman of faith. Having acquired a majority of her education in Baltimore City Public Schools System, Harrell is a proud alumna of Annapolis High School. Consequently, she earned an undergraduate degree in 2002 from Morgan State University. Then in 2004, she acquired a Master's Degree in Social Work from Widener University.

March 31, 2005, she accepted her call as a preacher of the gospel. Consequently, she earned a Master of Divinity in May 2015 from United Theological Seminary.

She is the owner and director of Transforming Lives Counseling Services (TLCS).

In 2021, Harrell made her authorship debut, with the release of Poems From The Heart, then weeks later after becoming one of sixty-two co-authors to collectively assemble *Soulful Affirmations: 365 Days Of Positive Thoughts And Lessons To Start Your Day.*

Married to Mr. Marvin Harrell, she is the mother of two "anointed and beautiful" children: Adah and Malachi.

Melissa can be reached for further information and preaching engagements at mpowell7611@yahoo.com or https://www.phenomenalwomanmin.com.

4

DUST FROM THE LION'S DEN

Vernice Cooper

With my cheek pressed firmly against the kitchen floor, I anxiously searched for hope between the seams of the vinyl tiles. There was something the cold floor offered me that a warm bed couldn't, so I gravitated there. I wasn't sure what would give in first, my body or my mind, but I didn't want to burden anyone with another trip to the Emergency room. As my heart pounded into the floor at 165 beats per minute and the nausea peaked to an all time high, all I could do was pray. But this prayer was different, this time I didn't ask God to rescue me from this episode. This time, I asked him to simply end the suffering as he saw fit, because I had reached my breaking point.

We were at the beginning of a *global pandemic*. Death was imminent. At least that's what I told myself as I searched for another life insurance policy that would set my family up for success in the event of my untimely departure. Many people reminded me I was lucky I didn't have COVID-19, and I should be grateful. However, this illness that had taken over my body was too severe and persistent to ignore. I was overwhelmed with fear and anxiety until I heard the spirit of the Lord say, "Really Vernice? Am I not the same God of Daniel?" Well yes, I thought to myself, but it's hard to compare yourself with a Bible character of big faith when mine had shrunken down to a mustard seed. The Bible illustrates Daniel as a strong, confident man who believed in God even after being thrown in a den with lions. *"Then the king commanded, and they brought Daniel, and cast him into the den of lions. Now the king spake and said unto Daniel, Thy God whom thou servest continually, he will deliver thee"* (Daniel 6:16 KJV). Yet, here I was in the den of defeat with no identifiable lion and questionable faith.

SURRENDER

I grew weary of fighting for relief. The nausea couldn't be contained with medication and the sleep deprivation was taking its toll. My healthcare provider routinely stated that all of my vitals, labs and X-rays were normal, leaving me questioning the validity of my health concerns. The psychological despair was catching up with my physical ailments. I'd had enough. I gave God permission to do his will. I knew that his will may have been death, but I had accepted my fate. Besides, there was a *global pandemic* plaguing the world, and I figured my death would be categorized as another pandemic casualty. Although my illness was unrelated to COVID-19, I had convinced myself that my family would be lucky enough to grieve among a multitude of grievers who'd lost loved ones. So I wallowed in this self pity and told myself I was practicing acceptance of the illness. But acceptance wasn't good enough. I heard the spirit of the Lord say, acceptance is far different then surrendering. Something shifted with this new revelation. I learned that surrendering wasn't about giving up, it was about giving in. It was yielding to God's Will and believing in His promises. So I stopped praying for relief, and I started praying for healing and expecting my vulnerability to open me up to new possibilities.

SEEK

"Ask, and it shall be given you; seek, and ye shall find; knock, and it shall be opened unto you:For every one that asketh receiveth; and he that seeketh findeth; and to him that knocketh it shall be opened" (Matthew 7:7-8 KJV)

I admired Daniel's trust in the Lord. Not only had he sought the Kingdom of God first, but it was engraved in the fabric of his existence. He sought after God in a way in which I wasn't familiar. He sought after my Granny Goose's God. The God that makes a way out of no way. I yearned for that relationship with God that they experienced, so I decided to seek Him for myself. I was no longer just praying for healing. I began praying for understanding, guidance and clarity. These prayers were different. There were long pauses of silence that I desperately wanted to be filled with answers. But God showed me something in those times. He showed me that He had given me clarity around my purpose long ago. He showed me that I had been sitting on my gifts for years, and He was waiting on a return on His investment in me.

Pursuing purpose in the midst of pain is next level faith. "Dear Lord, what else would you have me do while I'm here?" I asked. *'Finish your book, go back into spaces and speak healing over my people, be the light I assigned you to be,' He answered. Not for you, but for My name's sake.* I argued as I often did with God with His instruction. I thought to myself, how can I write when I'm constantly nauseous, sleep deprived and dizzy? I even tried a prayer of excuses and God responded with His sweet and precious silence. The absence of His voice was familiar. There are often times when I instruct my own children to do something and get tired of repeating myself, so I become silent. I began finding the spaces in the illness where things weren't so bad and began doing the things I was still capable of doing. My perspective began to shift yet again as

I sought the transformation I desperately wanted. I found a private holistic doctor who offered the curiosity, empathy and compassion my HMO providers lacked. I converted the late-night hours of sickness into productive writing sprints, finished a book project and started other entrepreneurial endeavors. Waiting until I was well was no longer a goal. I did it, sick and seeking.

SOAR

"And when he came to the den, he cried with a lamentable voice unto Daniel: and the king spake and said to Daniel, O Daniel, servant of the living God, is thy God, whom thou servest continually, able to deliver thee from the lions? Then said Daniel unto the king, O king, live forever" (Daniel 6: 20-21 KJV).

In the beginning of the illness, I spent so much time asking God why this was happening *to* me that I never considered maybe it was happening *for* me or for a greater purpose. The patience and spiritual maturity I developed was priceless. I worked feverishly with my holistic doctor, oftentimes with resistance to change until I realized it was the same resistance, I was offering God around pursuing my purpose. In the Bible, not only was Daniel released from the lion's den unharmed, but he became a living testament that changed the trajectory of his life and those around him. Daniel's story reminded me how faithful

God is. He will not only deliver you, but He will also propel you to new heights when you are operating in obedience and purpose. I still get sick from time to time, but I no longer fret because I understand that it is just dust from the lion's den and God is still on the throne.

ABOUT THE AUTHOR

Vernice Cooper is a dynamic empowerment speaker, coach, author, and a Licensed Marriage and Family Therapist who is determined to use her education and experience to inspire, motivate and transform lives. Her life experience of overcoming family addiction and trauma, paired with her professional experience fuels her passion to guide people, particularly women, out of a "Victimville" mentality. Using real-world examples, humor, and short storytelling, Vernice sheds light on how resilience transforms the way we live, love, and heal. Vernice currently works as a clinician specializing in Addiction Medicine and Recovery Services at Kaiser Permanente, owns her own consulting business, Joy Road Solutions LLC, and is a recovery coach.

Vernice is the author of best-selling, award-winning

Anthology, *Vacate Victimville: An Anthology for Hurt, Hope and Healing*, and author of her debut workbook, *Vacate Victimville: The Recovery Workbook*. Vernice is also a co-author for the Anthology, *The Breaking Point*.

Connect with Vernice

- http://www.vacatevictimville.net

5

TEAR-STAINED PILLOW

Teresa Ward

My body grappled with the notion of sleep every time my head hit the pillow. My heart raced and familiar tears flowed night after night unbeknown to my husband who slept right beside me. How could he rest so comfortably and not know that my heart was aching. I was angry. I was afraid. I was broken. I poured my life into this man and dreamt of a blessed and prosperous future with him as our children embarked upon their own journeys in life. My future expectations came to a screeching halt the night I watched the man I loved collapse on our bathroom floor. Within seconds his body was cold and unresponsive. My instant reaction was to yell, "Call 911" to my oldest daughter as I immediately began to pray for him. He aroused from his stupor and once again downplayed the severity of the situation. This place was familiar. We had been here once before and here we were yet again because of his unmanaged hypertension. The words, "I am done!" resonated within my heart as I watched him try to talk his way out of going to the hospital. If he didn't care, I wouldn't care! Gradually, my heart released him, but tears stained my pillow.

Hypertension was not a foreign word in our family. My mother-n-law died at the age of fifty-seven due to complications of hypertension. We certainly knew the risks of not taking prescribed medication properly. We were also well aware of the necessity of a healthy diet and exercise. By the grace of God, my husband was spared from death a few years prior. His unmanaged high blood pressure resulted in an aortic dissection, a five centimeter rip in his aorta. After a week in ICU and an additional week in a hospital room where even the slightest sneeze could have caused further complications, we returned home. I spent my nights listening at the sound of his breath and the beat of his heart as I lay my head on his chest. If he slept too soundly, I found myself touching his body feeling for signs of life. If his skin was cool to the touch of my fingertips, I experienced momentary panic. Fear slowly engulfed me as thoughts of my husband dying in his sleep tried to overtake me.

My husband's recuperation process was a daily task. A

task I willingly embraced as my desire was to see my man strong and healthy. However, the willingness was short-lived. He continued to make poor food choices and disregarded the necessity of his prescribed medication. I was going over and beyond to be the helpmeet God called me to be to no avail while he could care less. The descent of my heart towards him began to dictate my actions.

I managed to maintain a happy home to the best of my ability, yet internally, I was in turmoil. He indulged in choices that were not conducive to our future together, and I emotionally distanced myself from him. At the time, it was the only way I knew to calm the storm of raging fear within my heart. Eventually, I reached a plateau of stability in my mind, but it did not come without cost. My emotions were detached, and my husband was released from my heart. His wellbeing was of no concern to me at this point. Finally, I was free from the grips of fear, but nightly tears stained my pillow. Have you been there? Waiting, hoping, giving your all to someone who does not seem to care. How do you cope?

I was on autopilot, officially checked out and oblivious to the physical toll my decision was having on my body. Heart palpitations arrested my being and warm tears flowed instantly as my head touched my pillow every night. "God help me!" was the inaudible plea of my unhappy heart. My husband began to notice my lackluster smile and the insincerity of my responses to his slightest touch. I assured him time and time again that everything was fine. I loved my husband, but my emotional detachment blurred the lines. Convinced by my own voice of reasoning, I settled into my new normal.

My husband tried to improve, but fell prey to the lure of pork sandwiches and fried chicken. Compiled with overworking and self-medicating, he was a ticking time bomb and I was in la la land. A shell of myself, I was a woman in complete denial of her brokenness. The actual state of my existence was of no consequence to me until God revealed the true condition of my heart. A dear friend shared her dream about me that displayed my callous nonchalance when my husband was experiencing a crisis. Her words and look of bewilderment struck a chord in me. At that moment, I was fully aware of my Heavenly Father's displeasure. An immediate conviction flooded my heart and within my soul, I quietly asked God to forgive me. The brief dream she shared was an answer to the inaudible plea that took place in the night hours as I lay on my tear stained pillow. How many times have you cried out to God? Rest assured, he hears the righteous and delivers them. "The righteous cry, and the Lord heareth, and delivereth them out of all their troubles" (Psalm 34:17 KJV).

I needed intervention. Unwittingly, desperation was my

navigation instead of the Word of God. I attributed my brokenness to my husband's stubbornness and insensitivity, but in actuality, I was broken because I neglected to surrender my fears to God, my Father. In total abandonment of my will, I yielded my human frailties to Jehovah Rapha and he operated on my heart. The Word of God became my armor of protection. "For God hath not given us the spirit of fear; but of power, and of love, and of a sound mind" (2 Timothy 1:6 KJV) and "Beloved, I wish above all things that thou mayest prosper and be in health, even as thy soul prospereth" (3 John 1:2 KJV) became my mantra.

Poor choices were still evident in my husband's life, but I leaned on God instead of succumbing to fear. When his pressure escalated between skipping his medication and eating unhealthy meals, he self-prescribed his dosage as a cure all to the hypertension. However this time, his collapse on the bathroom floor proved it was not in his favor. He overdosed on his medication and his pressure dropped dangerously low. Fervently, I prayed as he lay unconscious. The fragility of life ignited flames of fear in my heart as he was again at death's door. "I don't care! I am done!" resounded in my thoughts. Feelings of despair tried to resurface, but my surrender was to God. I was strengthened and pressed beyond the anger and frustration.

My husband recovered, and it became obvious; I could not change a grown man. However, I would let my life be an example. I embraced the task of creating a healthy lifestyle plan regardless of my husband's personal choices. My meals were complete opposite of his. The more I indulged in healthy eating habits, the more he would complain about how much better my food looked in comparison. Eventually, we started walking together, riding bikes and eating healthy meals together. As time transpired, he made better food choices and took his medication as prescribed. Imagine my surprise when we found ourselves in an emergency room with the doctors telling me that my husband needed immediate transport via helicopter to St. Francis due to a brain hemorrhage.

A familiar situation was once again thrust upon me, but this time I was different. Fear did not grip my heart. (Philippians 4:6 KJV), "And the peace of God, which passeth all understanding, shall keep your hearts and minds through Christ Jesus," graced my life. I took a deep breath; communed with my Heavenly Father, made necessary phone calls and spoke the Word of God over my husband. I surrendered it all to Him. "Cast thy burden upon the Lord, and he shall sustain thee: He shall never suffer the righteous to be moved" (Psalm 55:22 KJV).

I was no longer the fearful brokenhearted woman who was angry and afraid of losing her husband. My trust was in the Lord. "Trust in the Lord with all thine heart" (Psalm 3:5a KJV). Needless to say, my husband was miraculously blessed by God. My Father intervened and healed him just like he intervened and healed my self-imposed brokenness. I am forever grateful for His love towards me. "Behold what manner of love the Father has bestowed upon us" (1 John 3:1a KJV).

What circumstances have you allowed to break your heart? Are fears holding you back from surrendering to God? The same God who healed my heart is the same God who can heal yours.

Surrender to God and trust Him for the miraculous!

ABOUT THE AUTHOR

Teresa Ward is an author, educator, entrepreneur, non-profit director and ordained evangelist. She authored a children's book, *Busy Little Anthony* and co-authored an anthology, *The Breaking Point*. In 2022, she will release a series of Bible memory journals and a children's book, *I Like Me.*

Teresa embraces the opportunity to work with children in kindergarten and first grade as an interventionist. She believes every child has the potential to succeed in the right environment.

Teresa Ward earned her associate and bachelor's degree of Ministry from International College of Bible Theology. As co-founder and director of operations for Love of the Truth International, Teresa strives to live, love and serve like Christ within her community and beyond by creating and implementing programs to impact, strengthen and empower the lives of underserved children and families.

As a writer, Teresa favors personal journaling and penning spoken word poetry.

She acknowledges her life as a hiker from heaven (heavenly hiker) set apart to live a healthy and consecrated life to the honor and glory of her Heavenly Father, one day at a time. She enjoys long nature hikes, recreating vegan and vegetarian recipes and juices in her kitchen, making cherished memories with her family, and being Nana to her precious grandbaby.

Teresa is married to Karl Ward. They are the chosen parents of three creative blessings from God and grandparents to a beautiful granddaughter. She currently resides in Memphis, TN.

Connect with Teresa Ward

- https://www.teresaannward.com
- www.Instagram.com/heavenlyhiker
- https://www.tiktok.com/@heavenlyhiker
- www.Facebook.com/heavenlyhiker
- teresaakward@gmail.com

6

A SILENT KILLER

Sondra King

It's the little *big things* that have the tendency to gradually eat away at your soul. Somehow it becomes questions of how? Why? Should I? And how did it lead up to this? You then begin to question your own choices. Your own sanity. It seems justifiable, and now becomes a matter of you against you. For me, it all began about six months after marriage. You start to notice those little red flags and simply begin forming a reason to ignore them. Does the good always outweigh the bad? Do you love him? I think these were my most pivotal questions. The deal-breaker questions were "What will people say or think? Is it all in my head, perhaps? Or will it change? I believe those mental thoughts have a way of holding you hostage in your own body.

Pens and needles became the norm. Good days became convincing myself that things were looking up. We have history, or we can simply make it work. Learned behavior becomes your enemy. Telling yourself today was a good day becomes your sanity. Somehow your faith begins to get questioned, tested, mocked, and judged. Days become weeks, weeks become months, and months become years. Eventually years become an eternity. At least what feels like an eternity. It's been almost ten years now. It all became a blur. You find yourself simply existing but not living. Everyday you slowly become a killer. You start to look at him differently. You don't like the person you've become when you look into the mirror.

Blaming yourself feels comforting. Sleeping becomes obsolete. I began to internalize thoughts of pain and mental anguish. You cry when everyone else is asleep. You put on a happy face for the kids, your family, and for those looking inward. Then I began to wonder when will all of this just end already? His loving voice turned into harsh words. "Ours" became "his." Protection becomes survival. Gentleness becomes vindictive. Affection turns into spite. He becomes a stranger, and you become the enemy. My prayer life seemed to be depleted. I have faith, but I'm struggling. I needed answers. I'm doing everything in my power to hold it together as a wife. Everything familiar became the unknown. Our mornings, days, and nights became word fights. Communication slowly became silence. Day in and day out. Sunrise to sunset. Love is questioned. Was it just feelings? A familiarity perhaps? His behavior became acceptable to me. This once gentle person becomes a monster. He's now always angry, bitter, spiteful and resentful. The time had come to make a change!

I needed to get out. I prayed and prayed. As I laid down that night, I asked God two simple questions. "God what do I need to do?" and "God what am I going to do?" My father was a Pastor, and I didn't want to bring him to shame, my family, nor myself. After all, everyone in the past that he'd married never ended up in divorce. No pressure, right? I remember going to bed with a soaked pillow because I was mentally drained. My physician had prescribed me sleeping pills just so I could sleep. I never knew what person I was dealing with on a day-to-day basis anymore. We tried counseling which ended up terribly. I was at my wits end. Everyday he became more and more disrespectful. Colder. I knew it was time to get out. And fast! I came up with a plan.

My workdays began to become a bit challenging. He would block my vehicle in on purpose so I couldn't get to work. Or anywhere for that matter. Things started to get very spiteful. He would intentionally hide car keys, remove house keys, food, and even day to day essentials needed. More days had gone by. It turned into a couple of weeks. I began pretending just to satisfy him and his ego. As I laid down crying once again, I heard God's voice.

God simply said, Sondra, either you're going to trust me or keep allowing this to happen. His statement then became my question. What are you going to do? You have a choice. I felt instantly at peace. God was just waiting on me. I started to execute my plans to leave. Mental abuse can be just as lethal as physical. It slowly eats away at you. The next day I began secretly packing and hiding things. You learn how to improvise very quickly. When he left the house, I was unbothered. I used that time to pack. To plan. To make calls and arrangements without his knowledge. I got an apartment in my name and had my daughter occupy it to make things less obvious. Things were finally coming together. I started moving things out slowly when he wasn't there.

Another week had passed. He finally caught me on the run. He told me he would do better, seek more counseling, etc. I told him I had made a decision, and I was leaving. Then came the monster. He said I wasn't leaving, He tried to hold me down so I couldn't leave. The kids came in, so it made it easy to exit. Once I left, he tried to convince me to stay. To come back. He offered to continue to do whatever it took. My father counseled us again. I was then staying at my apartment that he had no knowledge of. I wanted to make sure I was doing the right thing. How absurd was that? Things changed, but only temporarily. He only used it as a mind game. To toy with me. I wasn't the same person anymore. My tolerance became low. I learned how not to be a victim. His words no longer affected me. I finally learned how to start living and not existing. I left again for the last time. And I knew I wasn't going to ever return.

More weeks had gone by. He started coming on my job, calling non-stop, popping up at church. Doing things to try to convince me that he had changed. It was all a lie. I knew he hadn't changed. Behind closed doors, threats were made. All of a sudden, things had started happening to my vehicle. I knew he was behind it. I had gotten security involved at my job. I would take alternate routes home to ensure I wasn't being followed. I blocked his calls, but he would somehow find a way to get through. I remember our last conversation. He told me he had changed once again. He tried convincing me that things would be different if I came back. All of the things that I had asked him to do when we were together at home, he did them. He was talking in third person. As if I were back with him. I told him if he did them when I left, it just proved that he could've done them all along. He simply chose not to. Not because he couldn't, but because he wanted to prove a point. That he was in control. It's amazing how freedom becomes clarity. And peace becomes life. You never really realize it until it becomes a reality. You can now answer the questions that you were once unsure of. I now had a peace that I couldn't explain.

A Silent Killer was me. I was killing myself mentally, physically, emotionally, and spiritually. I had given it my all. But decided to give it to God. Sometimes we can slowly kill ourselves. We don't need a "thing." God wants us to live life abundantly. It's not his will for us to suffer in silence. To keep things bottled up until we're physically ill or on the verge of a mental break. It's been about four years now. Everything has changed. My residence, my phone number, my employment, my vehicle, and my relationship with Christ. It is better than I would have ever imagined for myself. I do things that bring me joy. I no longer accept things that don't serve my purpose. Sometimes you have to let go of the things, the people, and the situations that simply don't serve you. Never allow people to devalue you. Know your worth. Know that there's hope. Trust God. Have faith. There's always a light at the end of the tunnel. Sometimes you have to take that leap of faith, even when you don't know the outcome. And trust that God will do the rest. Your tears turn back into laughter. Your broken heart becomes mended. You are now living and not existing. He is now a part of my past. Not my future. I broke all ties. The killer becomes free. Never allow someone or something to take your voice. Don't kill your dreams, aspirations, or purpose. God has such a great plan for your life. Just trust his process.

ABOUT THE AUTHOR

Author Sondra King has co-authored an Anthology, *The Breaking Point*. She describes herself as an educator and entrepreneur by profession, an author by purpose, and is also a health/wellness lifestyle blogger. Her blog page can be found at www.simplysondrak.com, or you can contact her by email at simplysondrak@gmail.com.

Sondra is currently continuing her education in hopes of becoming a Health and Wellness Coach. Sondra was inspired to share her *My Daily Prayer* devotion that was written over twenty years ago. She wrote this devotion at a time where she needed Christ the most. Writing has always been her way of escape, expression, therapy, and inspiration. Not only is writing her passion, it is her purpose! *My Daily Prayer* helps you to focus on the importance of establishing some one-on-one time with God. It also teaches you how to carve out time daily from our busy lives, in order to spend those quiet moments with Jesus. Prayer is vital and *My Daily Prayer* provides simple reminders, along with scriptures and note sections. Additionally, she continues to inspire others through her writing. She has recently written a sequel to this devotion entitled My Daily Prayer II which will be released early in 2022 and available on Amazon and also by audiobook.

Sondra currently resides in Lakeland, TN and is the proud mother of four children and three grandchildren.

Connect with Sondra

- Facebook.com/SondraKing or Simplysondrak
- Twitter.com/simplysondrak
- Instagram.com/sondrakking or simplysondrak
- sondrak602@gmail.com

7

MY BREAKTHROUGH INTO MANHOOD

Santos Howard

"Every man has a secret sorrow which the world knows not; and often times we call a man cold when he is only sad." Henry Wadsworth Longfellow

This book forced itself on me while I was trying to write something else. It probably still bears the marks of the reluctance with which a great part of it was composed after pondering my life. I've had many breakthrough moments over the years, and this one is pivotal in my transition to manhood. It defined who I was as a man and shaped my perception of life. Life before this breaking point was filled with misnomers about being a man. At the age of seventeen, I thought I was a man. After all, I did have a wife and a son. I was living on my own in another state and thought taking care of my family was being a man.

The circumstances of my birth weren't unusual, but nonetheless traumatic. My father was unknown to my family. He had a reputation for being a procurer of women. My mother didn't tell anyone about him; that was by design I'm sure on his part. The fateful day my family met him was the day we were leaving abruptly and without any warning for California. Cleveland, Ohio is where I was birthed and didn't return for forty-five years.

California is where I was raised by a single mother. Like most boys in my generation, our mothers raised us, shaped our identities and our ideology of the world. I was influenced by my mother's boisterous communication style and her domineering ways. She was in my opinion a womanist. Men didn't get a whole lot of respect from her, so I had an adverse view of men. I didn't respect men. They were not to be respected or trusted; I was antagonistic towards men only in my mind. I couldn't beat them up. I challenged men vehemently in my mind, attitude, posture. There wasn't much a man could tell me.

Buried in the recesses of our minds are memories that we suppress and continue about our daily lives until we must come face to face with the pain. The sequence of events that took place were painful, unsettling, and of extraordinary proportion. This chapter alone isn't adequate to share my story in depth.

THE REJECTION

Typically, fathers weren't present and mine, purposefully, wasn't in my life. I remember when I was five years old, I was playing outside by myself in front of my grandmother's, affectionately known as MaMo, house. My father had a friend who lived across the street from my grandmother. He would visit his friend often. This day I remember vividly because someone said to my father "That's your son over there playing." He responded, *"That's not my son, that's a trick's baby."* I heard it and I just kept playing. It took forty-two years for me to realize the effects of what I heard my father say in his rejection of me. My father's rejection affected me in ways I never knew.

I was preemptive, I disqualified myself from opportunities of building relationships with people, expecting rejection. Oftentimes, rejection would happen which affected the release of my expression of me. Very often I was accused of being aloof and arrogant.

I didn't realize I was carrying his rejection of me all those years. I had an emotional breakdown over his rejection of me. Five years ago, I was in prayer one morning when God showed me the incident with my father. It was a melancholic moment, a day of reckoning. It put in perspective for me where the seed of rejection started. I cried like a five-year-old would cry that fell and hurt himself severely. The adage, "sticks and stones may break my bones, but words will never hurt me," is a lie. Words hurt even when we don't realize it.

MY CONVERSION

Having been enlightened by the power of the Holy Spirit, I accepted Jesus as my personal savior. The spiritual awakening I had experienced started a shift in my mind, My soul was struggling with the persona I had developed in my mother's house. One day while at home with my ex-wife and son, I was exuding what I now call my mother's female energy. I was being boisterous with my communication, being tyrannical and beating my chest about being the man of my house! In that instance, something significant happened. It was like I had an out–of–body experience in fact I did have an out–of–body experience. I saw myself standing there being overly emotional. Out of control, nothing manly about me, timid, and lacking confidence. God spoke to me and said, "This isn't who I created you to be. I'm going to teach you how to be a man."

It was at that moment my breakthrough into manhood began. He showed me where my point of reference for manhood was lacking masculinity. He used my older friend to show me masculinity. A man's man, the leader of his home, and an elder in the church of our Lord and savior Jesus Christ. What I learned from him at eighteen years old shaped my philosophy even until today. The process of becoming a man is a forever evolving process. You're always developing as a man, there are some principles that are foundational to manhood. The first thing God made me aware of was myself and what that looked like. It wasn't a good look. He started reshaping my self-awareness. My power as a man was realized when I understood that it wasn't in how loud I was and how hard I could beat my chest. My power was in my ability to control myself, and my emotions, while calming the emotions of my family. God showed me that self-awareness, is the seat of the soul. Let's examine the *Self-Awareness* theory, developed by Shelley Duval and Robert Wicklund in their 1972 landmark book, "A Theory of Objective Self-awareness, states that when we focus our attention on ourselves, we evaluate and compare our current behavior to our internal standards and values. There are five general things that need to be addressed in self-awareness:

- Your history
- Culture
- Self-reflection
- Knowledge of self
- Living in your truth

Allow me to explain: *Your history* is the study of your human past as it is described by your family. It's the past with all its complicated choices and events. It is the influence of participants dead, and history told by those that are present with us today. God uses our history to help define our present life situations. Without a history, you have no future.

Culture is a critical dynamic of self-awareness. It helps define your personality, characteristics, and self-concept. Culture gives you a sense of connectedness to those around you and your behavior; you'll be really surprised how your culture can affect your behavior. God started changing my culture, my self-concept started to evolve. He had already moved me away from the culture that defined my self-actualization.

Your *knowledge of self* is your thought–life. The aforementioned factors, history, culture, and self-reflection can and will affect your thought–life. Your thought–life affects your beliefs, and your beliefs affect your life. God started teaching me how to manage my thoughts. I'm reminded of a Biblical text written by the Apostle Paul:

"Finally, brethren, whatsoever things are true, whatsoever things are honest, whatsoever things are just, whatsoever things are pure, whatsoever things are lovely, whatsoever things are of good report; if there be any virtue, and if there be any praise, think on these things" (Philippians 4:8 KJV).

After all, keeping it real with myself; *living in my truth* was the cohesion I needed to breakthrough into manhood. I learned my purpose as a man was defined in my realness with myself. I had to create a new reality. If I can't exist in my reality, I can't be a man. If I can't keep it real with me, I can't keep it real with anyone. Breaking Points are defining moments in our lives. They tell us that it's time to accept our reality and breakdown the barriers that caused us to lose our identity, our peace, our freedom, love for ourselves. All those things that come to weaken our souls and cause us to accept less than what God intended for our lives.

I broke through my Breaking Point on seemingly broken pieces. Nonetheless, I broke through all the negative experiences that made me who I was. I stood on those broken pieces with a word from God, that Word was "This isn't who I created you to be." God didn't create you to be a happenstance, or an afterthought. The steps of a good man are ordered by God; your steps are ordered by God. I encourage you to *breakthrough*, live your best life, don't sacrifice anymore of you than you're not willing to give up freely.

ABOUT THE AUTHOR

A Pastor, entrepreneur, scholar, speaker, and aspiring theologian, he is the Founder of LIFE Church in Suisun, CA. A ministry dedicated to building God's Kingdom one family at a time. His life is dedicated to guiding people to a life of faith in Jesus Christ, then on to lives that are empowered and fully dedicated to God, through his passion for God's Word, which brings freedom and enlightenment. Santos has more than a decade of teaching and counseling experience, which enables him to reach others with warmth, transparency, and strength. He is a teacher, conference speaker, and mentor. Well-known for his business acumen, he's a serial entrepreneur with a passion for the "art of the deal."

Santos is a life-long learner with a certificate in Literary Theory and Criticism from the University of Oxford, a certificate of Theology in Ministry from Princeton Theological Seminary, a bachelor's degree in Biblical Studies from Grace Bible College, a Master of Theology from Ecumenical Theological Seminary, and a Doctorate from Spirit of Truth Theological Seminary.

When Santos isn't studying, ministering, speaking, or brokering a business deal, he enjoys spending time with his wife of thirty years, Debbie, traveling, and experiencing different cultures all over the world. They have four adult children and seven grandchildren. He also loves action movies and is a loyal Lakers and 49ers fan.

Connect with Santos

- Email: Santosho5@myself.com
- FB: https://www.facebook.com/santos.howard
- IG: @lifechurch

8

MY SEASON OF PURPOSE

Judy A. Hewitt

"To everything there is a season, and a time to every purpose under the heaven," (Ecclesiastes 3:1 KJV).

As I look back over the seasons of my life, which was not straight forward, I had to learn to lean into the twists, turns, ups and downs. At the age of fifty-nine, I finally decided that this journey did not serve me anymore. I had more years behind me than in front of me and relocated back to Florida and took my life back.

I was done with living for everyone else and helping them fight their demons, which left me paralyzed to fight my own. Done putting everyone's needs before my own. At the end of the day, my cup was empty.

Other's pain, hurts, and sorrows were that...other people's pain and not my own.

That was the day I was at my breaking point. I cried out to the Lord! Just like King David, I had to encourage myself in the Lord (1Samuel 30:6 KJV)

SEASON OF WILDERNESS

You see I was being held captive by painful memories of my past. It always pleased me to be needed. It really pricked at my heartstrings to see someone in distress. I did not know people were in your life for a reason, season, or a lifetime. I can honestly say I was at war with myself. It felt like I was a robot; my life was on automation. I woke up every morning and set out to work only to pay the bills and wake up and do it all over again. Working to survive during this season of my life, self-care was not on my list of priorities.There was never time for personal pleasures or time to simply enjoy life. Was I a work alcoholic?

My answer would be *yes*. If I had to be honest, I would say that this was modeled behavior passed down to me. With that, I struggled with understanding self-love and imparting and sharing love, because it was not given. As a result, I desired that my immediate family and everyone in my community received love and appreciation from me. So often we overcompensate—trying to correct or make amends for our weaknesses. I put myself last and didn't love myself. It was easier for me to pour from an empty cup just to make those around me happy. Don't get me wrong, I loved pouring and giving to those near and dear to my heart. It brought me great joy. But did it help my esteem? Did it bring healing and restoration to me? Did it relieve all the pains of my past?

I can recall a therapy session in which I was instructed to look at myself in the mirror and repeat, "I love me." I could not do it. The brokenness I was experiencing on the inside was more spiritual than it was personal. My past had been buried for so long that it rooted itself in misery, brokenness, and unworthiness. I was focused on all the wrong things. Once I started experiencing some health challenges, it led me to believe that time was no longer on my side; life was passing me by. There's a difference between living and existing, and I was not living my life at all. It hit me; I was powerless up against what I was battling. I was stuck in the role of Martha. Martha, the character in the book of (Luke 10:38-42 KJV). As they were visited by Jesus, Martha's focus was on the busy things in life distracting her from relevance of what Jesus wanted to pour into her. Mary, on the other hand, knew to sit at the feet of Jesus so that she did not miss out on the opportunity of His pouring. I could relate to Martha's side of the story, because I, too, was focused on the busy things.

Season of Restoration

Once I relocated, I knew to win in this season in life, I had to purposefully focus on the Word of God and love myself. I returned to doing things that made me happy and brought me joy. Walking along the beach, watching a sunset, art, music, poetry, and journaling. I was reconnecting with me. Doing it for me symbolized my living the life I wanted. A life of truth. A life of discovery. A life of healing, restoration, and acceptance. A life of new beginnings. A life of purpose. They say that purpose is hooked to a destination, and I had landed. I was back in Florida where it all began. I believe that God's intentions for our lives is His final decision. Meaning the purpose and plans that God has for your life does not change. He does not rewrite the story after we journey down the paths of life we take. If anything, He redirects us, and even then, we always end up right back where we belong.

Once I was back in Florida, there was no one to nurture, fix, or assist. It was just me and God. I soon discovered that He wanted alone time with me. When you think about it, how awesome is it for God to order your footsteps to a place where He can have you all to Himself. I had been the savior for so many when I needed the one and only savior, Jesus Christ.

In this season, I recommitted myself to Him, to focus more on Him, His word, and the plans He had for my life. I was totally isolated from everything and everyone because a few months after my return, the world faced a pandemic in 2020. We were quarantined and, for me, it was another opportunity to be alone with God. Lord, it's just me and you I whispered. During this time, everything was resetting and the world as we knew it had drastically changed. God was resetting everything around us. I felt as if what was happening to the world was happening to me spiritually. God was resetting me and my life. The reset reconnected me with my love for writing and journaling; I also found myself and my purpose. I even rekindled my love for the arts. Everything began to flow effortlessly, and doors were opening. It was as if the Holy Spirit had taken me by the hand and was personally guiding me through my reset experience. All my needs were being met—one after another. He was truly giving me the desires of my heart, and I saw Him in the details.

SEASON OF WINNING

My vision and destiny became crystal clear. The dots of life were beginning to make sense and connect like never. It was in the reset that I realized that everything—and I do mean everything—that I had been through was necessary, and all part of His plan. I know that God has more in store for me, and I am patiently waiting. I speak from experience when I say that there is NO limit to what God can do! I now know that I am walking out the purpose and plan (Jeremiah 29:11 KJV) that God has for my life. I know without a shadow of doubt that I am grounded and filled with purpose.

Whatever season in life you find yourself, I say to you never give up and always trust the process. It's not too late! You aren't behind. You're exactly where you need to be, and every step and experience is necessary. Never lean on your own understanding—and if you feel like He is no longer with you, go back to where you left Him. And you will find Him. His grace is sufficient and know that your impossible is possible with God. As a matter-of-fact, God is comfortable with the impossible. That is where He shows up.

I have learned my past failures cannot hinder my fruitfulness. I had to change my confession. My life's journey did not change my identity. As is written in Isaiah 54: 4(KJV). Fear not, I will not be put to shame, I will forget the shame of your youth, and will not remember the reproach of thy widowhood. He is faithful! If he said it! that settles it, and it shall come to pass.

ABOUT THE AUTHOR

Author Judy A Hewitt has co-authored an anthology, The Breaking Point. She's also co-author of Amazon #1 bestselling anthology, For Such a Time as This. She has been spotlighted in several magazine and had the honor of speaking on various radio shows to promote and discuss her journey and books.

She has a Bachelor of Science in Business Administration. Her career spans over eighteen years as a Case manager. An admitted writer, poet and lover of music and art, Hewitt is committed to using her God given gift to improve the lives of those touched by her writing.

Originally a native of Trinidad and Tobago, she now calls Florida home. Devoted to her four grandchildren and in the memory of her son Ronald C Hewitt, she writes.

Connect with Judy A. Hewitt

- www.judyahewitt.com
- www.facebook.com/Judy Ann Hewitt

9

SINGLE MOTHER TO THE STREETS

Lisa Humdy

"How did I get here? This is not how my life is supposed to end." I hear the click click of the gun being cocked and placed next to my temple. "You either going to be working for me or get the hell out of my city." I closed my eyes begging and praying for God to protect me and save me from this situation so I can get back to my daughters. My sister who was pregnant with her first child was watching my girls for me as she thought I was working my night job as a bottle service girl for private parties.

There was a tap on the window "Ma'am, is everything okay here?" Thank you, Jesus. It was a police officer. I rolled my window down and before I could speak, he said, "Ma'am, please step out of the car." Clearly the officer could see me crying and shaking. I opened the door slowly, not sure if Slim was going to shoot me. And as I got out and walked towards the back of the car, the other officer yelled "He has a gun!"

The officers arrested Slim, and now I could breathe a little bit more. "Ma'am, did he hurt you in anyway? Do you need any medical attention?" I could see Slim staring at me and mouthing "I'm going to get you for this," as they place him into the back of the patrol cars. "No, officer, I'm fine. You came just before anything was going to happen."

I was still shaking and finding it hard to focus. The world was turning black on me. "Ma'am, we have a few questions. Let's sit you down so you can relax a little. You're safe now." I wish those words were true. Being safe, I know now more than ever, I need to watch my back and get myself out of this. I need to get home, but where is home?

After answering all the questions for the officers, they released me and made sure I was calm enough to drive. It was late, and I just wanted to get home and hold my daughters. I really thought this was the night I was going to die. As I'm driving down the street getting closer to my house, I keep hearing the sound of the gun being cocked over and over with Slim's voice yelling at me. I felt like I'm about to be sick.

I finally pulled up in front of my house, and once I placed the car in Park, I just sat there and cried. "Lord, I don't know why you saved me, but I'm thankful for you blessing me to come home to my girls." Walking into the house, I just lay in the bed with my daughters with tears running down my face, so thankful to hold them in my arms again.

When I look back at my life, it really all began with my grandfather telling me I will never amount to anything. These words have haunted me for years, and probably why even today, it's hard for me to see something all the way through to the end. The man that raised me mentally damaged my mind, having me believe I was a failure and success was something I would never achieve. Even with him deceased, his words continue to haunt me every day. His words kept me silent and always made me feel weak. That my voice, my thoughts, or anything I had or wanted to share was not important. It didn't matter how hard I tried my best for him, it was never enough. I was not important, so why would anyone else see me as important or care about what I had to say.

Those same words led me to settle for a man who never loved or wanted me. He only wanted me to have his children and live his life as he pleased. Consistently in and out of jail ever since my oldest daughter was two months old. This man cheated on me numerous times, denying it while giving me STDs multiple times. The mental abuse, really wanting me to believe that I couldn't do better than him. But he didn't want a family. He wanted the fast money, the streets and any woman that showed him attention. The only blessing from him was my beautiful daughters, who deserved so much better than this pattern of life I was choosing to remain in. While their father was in and out of jail, I struggled to make ends meet and provide for my children.

Asking my family for help and support was something I just could not do. My pride stood in the way. I could hear my grandfather still saying, "You will never amount to nothing. This is all you're going to be. Just worthless." I hid the fact that I was hurting so badly from my children and my family. I never told anyone this dark secret of mine. It takes a lot to be vulnerable and open up when things in life always seem to go left field no matter how many attempts you try to make things go right.

My daughters deserved better, and they were the only thing I could think about: giving them a better life by all means necessary. So the following morning I sucked up my pride and made the call that I was dreading to make for so many years and called my mother, tears streaming down my face. "Hi, Mom. I need help. Can me and the girls please come home?" I'm so thankful for the struggles and life lessons I survived. It definitely helped mold me into the woman I am today. But if I had a chance to change anything in my past, it would be to learn to swallow my pride and reach out to ask for help sooner than suffering through trials I unnecessarily could have avoided.

However, I had to learn to forgive and make peace with those who have hurt me. Starting with my grandfather. He made me silence and not use my voice. I decided at this moment his words will no longer hold me captive in negativity, and I will not remain stuck in a toxic mindset. But, instead, I will use his words to fuel me to fight for a better life for myself and my daughters. No longer will I allow others to use or mistreat me, I am stronger than I realize "Strength and honor are her clothing; she shall rejoice in time to come" (Proverbs 31:25-KJV). This was my breakthrough, I released myself from the pain, hurt, suffering and fears of my past. I decided that not only do my daughters deserve better, but so do I. I am worthy, I am enough, I am smart, and I am confident. The shell I once was trapped in is now broken, and I have learned to spread my wings like a butterfly and soar to my greatness. I no longer allow others to speak over me, I no longer remain silent, and most importantly I fell in love with myself. My life turned for the better when I discovered who Lisa was. Ready to step out into this world and chase my dreams, I started network marketing and met some very powerful and successful entrepreneurs who have mentored me to pursue this life of success. They also taught me that not everyone will support me and my dreams, but to never give up on them. Only Lisa can make Lisa happy and only Lisa can believe in Lisa. "She is Strong." Through prayer and hard work, I've finally made it to a career that I've always wanted. As a Supervisor in Recruiting Operations, I'm leading others to be great, pushing them to strive for their dreams and showing others success is achievable. One of the most courageous decisions you'll ever make is to finally let go of what is hurting your heart and soul.

Does my story resonate with you? Has anyone ever spoken words over your life that have either hurt you or damaged your spirit? This is what I did to heal and persevere.

ABOUT THE AUTHOR

Lisa Humdy grew up in her grandparents' home with her brother. She went to Catholic schools through her sophomore year and spent her last two years in a public school. She went on to attend the University of Phoenix. She is the mother of three beautiful daughters and grandmother to two grandsons.

Lisa has fifteen years of experience in Human Resources Information Systems specializing in Talent Acquisition. She joined Pacific Gas and Electric Company in 2016 as a Senior Recruitment Coordinator responsible for revising existing policies and creating new guidance onboarding documents. In 2018, Lisa became the Recruiting Operations Supervisor in the east San Francisco Bay Area. Her new position supports Human Resource initiatives, and she supervises the work of assigned Recruiting Coordinators.

Lisa spends time away from her corporate job as an entrepreneur for various network marketing platforms. She is a diverse, accomplished leader in her community and has garnered the respect of her peers and co-workers.

Lisa started journaling in high school, capturing her thoughts, dreams, and emotions. Although life has not always been what she hoped for, she is ready to share her truth in this new collaboration, *The Breaking Point*. It is her debut as a published author. She hopes that her chapter will provide comfort and encouragement to those on similar life paths and believes in her future. Dream bigger!

Connect with Lisa
Lisa is happy to hear your comments. Contact her at lisahumdy@gmail.com.

10

A JOURNEY FROM PAIN TO PURPOSE

Diana Smith

"Pain serves a purpose. Without it you are in danger. What you cannot feel you cannot take care of. "

-Rebecca Solnit

Have you ever asked yourself this question, " Why me"? I am sure you have. For sure I have, a few times in my life. In 2008, my journey was taking a turn for the better. It was the pivotal moment where I decided to own who I was, stand in my truth and love the hell out of myself unapologetically. I was no longer saying yes just to fit in or keep a guy to stick around. You see, somewhere along my childhood leading up to adulthood, I stopped loving who I was. I did not recognize the woman looking back at me in the mirror. I am love and worthy of love. After multiple failed relationships, it was time for me to deal with me on a real level. One summer afternoon, as I sat alone at the kitchen table watching my three beautiful daughters play in the front yard, tears began to stream down my face. I am thinking to myself, why me? Dealing with back-to-back heartaches seemed so unfair. First, a divorce from my forever person—at least that is what I thought at the time. Then getting into a relationship two years later that would propel me towards my purpose.

In 2006, one beautiful Saturday night, out on the town with my girlfriend Raquel, she looks over at me as I was driving and recommended a dating site to find my "Mr. Right." I laughed and said, "No way! I have never done that before." We both started laughing. After returning home that evening, I began to think about what my girlfriend said about dating online, and decided to entertain the idea. I created a profile on this dating platform and began receiving hits almost immediately. A little creepy at first, but the attention was nice. Before logging off that evening, I had a date scheduled with Greg the following Friday.

Greg and I met for dinner at La Neves, a restaurant local to the both of us. That night seemed perfect. As we gazed into each other's eyes, nothing could prepare me for what was to come after meeting that night.

One night turned into two years, and it was not fun anymore. It started about nine months into our relationship, and the nice caring guy I met at the restaurant was slowly diminishing away. Greg had become possessive and controlling over me. At first, I thought it was cute until we visited my family out of state, and he cut our visit short. He had become jealous of a compliment I'd received from my sister's friend who was there when we arrived. On my way out the door, I hugged my sister goodbye, and Greg and I headed back on the road. It turned out to be the longest five-hour drive in my life. In retrospect, it was the most manipulative tactic I had ever experienced. The silent treatment was to teach me a lesson. It was Greg's way of punishing me. After a cycle of feeling ostracized in this connection, I would forgive him time and time again. But one evening, I suspected Greg of cheating, with both of us yelling at each other. He suggested we go for a drive. Nothing could have prepared me for what was about to happen. The spirited discussion ended with Greg threatening my life at gun point. I was shocked and went silent. Not wanting to upset Greg any further, I asked that he take me home. We both knew this would be the end of our relationship.

This moment was the turning point in my life. When I returned home, I fell to my bedroom floor crying and thanking God. He'd allowed me to escape what could have taken my life. This ordeal with Greg made me realize I had lost myself along the way and desperately wanted to rediscover who God created me to be. They say, hindsight is 20-20. Now looking back after fourteen years since my relationship drama with Greg, I was at peace, grateful that I had another chance to make right decisions not only in life but in love. At some point during my journey between going through a divorce, then dating a man who threatened my life, I forgot that I do matter. There are so many women who blame themselves for getting into bad relationships, but truth be told, a lot of times we go all in expecting to be swept off our feet. To hear how beautiful we are, and we begin to lose ourselves. Before you know it, we are codependent on our partner to make us happy and feel good about ourselves. But I had it all wrong. Being happy is an inside job. I should have never expected anyone to fill that void in my heart. In the summer of 2010, I rededicated myself to church and joined the women's ministry. There I met several women from all walks of life who shared their story like my own. Living in a cycle of broken relationships and seeking to rediscover who they were. I was in good company. I realized God truly had a purpose in the pain I'd endured. That He could turn my mess into a message to be a testament on how I overcame feeling worthless, unloved, and damaged, to being empowered to help other women overcome toxic connections to come out stronger on the other side.

Psalm 28:7 says, "The Lord is my strength and my shield;

my heart trusts in him, and he helps me. My heart leaps for joy, and with my song I praise him" (Psalm 28:7 NIV).

I had to trust God to give me strength, surrender, and grow through what I'd gone through. We know this is not always easy, but it is an important part of our journey to heal. There were four steps that were instrumental in helping me not only survive, but thrive and to live without fear and walk in faith to become the best version of myself. To walk in my truth unapologetically.

I have incorporated this four-step process to love and accept me for me again.

Step #1. Surrender

Have you ever found yourself trying to change your own flat tire as a woman? If you have, like me once or twice in your life, you realize that changing a tire is not something you can do successfully to make it to your destination. You may call a mechanic who has the tools to change your tire for you to drive away safely. Well, that is what surrender to me represents. It's giving up my way of doing things that's clearly not working. By me surrendering to God's plan for my life, I can trust that He's got my back. *Jeremiah 29:11, (NIV) says, For I know the plans I have for you," declares the Lord, "plans to prosper you and not harm you, plans to give you hope and a future.*

Step #2. Forgive Yourself

It is easy to blame yourself for the mistakes you've made along your journey, but we are human. Mistakes will happen. When you know better, you do better. I had to forgive myself for seeing the red flags while dating Greg, but chose to ignore them. It would have minimized the hurt I have gone through, but even the hurt was designed to help me grow. Forgiveness sets you free.

Step #3.Focus on the present, Not the past

It is funny how the past has a way of creeping back up in your life. Whether through reminiscing about the "good ole days" you've had or shuffling through photos when you were happy. But if you take a closer look, you realized your past brought more tears of sadness than happiness. Looking back on the past, I have cried more times than I want to admit. But today, I do not cry because I'm sad, I cry because I survived.

Step #4. Own Your Truth

One of the most daunting things to loving myself again was to own my truth. I can remember being embarrassed about my failed marriage, then falling into another relationship with a man who belittled me, tore me down, and threatened my life. Owning your truth speaks volumes. It means you are human. You had failures. A bad past does not equate to a bad life. I get that now. Owning my truth liberated me to become the best version of myself. Today, I share my truth to impact and empower women to know they can change the trajectory of their life, to know their self-worth to be a woman of purpose who is faithful, fearless, and free.

Woman of Purpose, You Do Matter.

ABOUT THE AUTHOR

Diana is a mom first, life coach, founder and host of the Love is Grace Podcast, and an Amazon bestselling author. She is a New Jersey native born and raised who has a love for dancing as a Zumba instructor when she is not speaking and motivating women to be relentless in their pursuit of self-discovery, self-love, and personal growth. Diana is a survivor of thyroid cancer and domestic abuse; she knows firsthand about trusting God and having unshakable faith.

She has three beautiful young adult daughters and enjoys spending time with her grandson. Diana is the author of You Matter, Self-care Journal and co-author of Women Crushing Mediocrity, Sisters Inspiring Sisters, Faith Leadership Finance, and her latest anthology The Breaking Point where she shares how she overcame a toxic relationship and allowed the pain to propel her towards her purpose with passion and perseverance.

Diana currently resides in the Washington DC Metropolitan Area. On her downtime' she can watch reruns of her favorite TV show Nashville like it is her first time. She is also the CEO of Inspired Motivationz LLC, a community of change to guide and empower women to step out of fear and walk in faith to be confident, successful and have the life they aspire to live.

Connect with Diana

- Website: www.dianasmith.co
- Instagram: www.Instagram.com/iamjusdiana
- Email: hello@dianasmith.co

11

EVACUATE – EVACUATE!!

Joanne Harte

Enough was enough! And I had had my full share of the "enoughs." Enough of the lies; enough of the criticisms; enough of the verbal and mental abuse; enough of the cheating. Enough of having to adjust myself to fit into his unstable world. I had bent all the way backwards in the hope that one day we could move forward. Did it make a difference? No—he mistook my forgiveness for weakness, and he had intended to ride me out. I was so mentally fragmented that I could not even recognize myself. My spirit was so broken I had no energy left, not even for me. Have you ever been so torn and tattered that it felt like you were about to lose your mind? Yes? Then you know it's not a fun place to be. It was not what I signed up for, and certainly not the way I could spend the rest of my life. I knew if I continued in that direction, I'd either be dead or badly wounded. After giving the best that I could, finally, I had gotten to my breaking point.

I remember it like it was only yesterday. That Saturday morning mid-September in 2015, at about 4:30 am, he had left for work. I made sure he was well out of the way before I made that phone call. "Come get me." It had come to the point where I had to make that uncomfortable call. "Please come get me." I had to get out. I had to escape. He had really hurt me. I felt utterly disrespected. The women, the lies, the deliberate verbal insults and mental abuse were more than too much. He wanted to be married, but still live as single. My breaking point finally came after seeing him that evening with the young lady on Utica Avenue in Brooklyn. That sealed the deal for me. It had gotten to the point where I felt as if I did not leave, I might hurt him if he didn't hurt me physically first. I had never felt that way before. Not about him or anyone else. I had always been someone who could forgive quickly. I never before struggled with forgiveness. But this time it was an up-hill battle. I had seen him with my own eyes.

In my line of work, I was constantly on the aircraft traveling to somewhere or the other. I knew that if I ever heard the captain say "Evacuate – Evacuate," it was a matter of life and death. It would be a scenario that warranted my jumping that ship without asking any questions. That was exactly how I felt in my spirit about the marriage. *Evacuate – Evacuate!* It was necessary to get out immediately for my own safety and sanity, and for the sanctity of the rest of my family members. I don't for one minute encourage divorce, but there are times when you have to escape the toxicity to save your own life. My escape, I believe, saved my life. I could breathe again.

I am so grateful to God for answered prayers. When I was in the middle of the pain and heartache, I kept praying, asking God to deliver me. One day walking down the road reminiscing on what had taken place, I told the Lord, "Lord, I prayed for your deliverance." He said to me, "Yes, you prayed for deliverance, and this is how I chose to deliver you. God is faithful. He delivered me indeed. In hindsight, that deliverance became my inflection point. It changed the trajectory of my life. I was free to live again. Of course, I had my moment of grief; but I am so appreciative that I got out alive.

My community of close family and friends were my shoulders to cry on. My brothers, sisters, my daughter and her husband, all stood by my side in that season. They listened to my venting. They cried with me, sat with me and most of all, they prayed for me.

It is so vital to surround yourself with faithful like-minded people. Your koinonia – the kind of community that will be delighted to lend support when you need it; the kind of friends you can confide in. I thank God for my folk daily.

Since then my life has taken to new heights, to Higher Altitudes. I am in a place of pursuing my purpose with passion. I am a woman on a mission to help others elegantly escape their own toxic situations, whether it is in marriage, on the job or even in their own mindset.

If ever you find yourself in a place where you feel stifled and stagnated, where your voice cannot be heard and your viewpoint in not validated, my word to you is that you don't have to remain where you are not welcomed. Who wants to be where they are only tolerated, but not appreciated and valued? Not me! And I am tempted to think neither do you. You are valuable. You are valuable to God. Don't allow anyone to tell you otherwise or treat you as less. Refuse to believe their lies when they say, "You're too old, you're too ugly, you're too obese, not educated enough." Refuse to accept the labels they want to attach to you. Let me remind you who you are—who God says you are:

> But ye are a chosen generation, a royal priesthood, a holy nation, a peculiar people; that ye should shew forth the praises of him who hath called you out of darkness into his marvelous light" (1 Peter 2:9 KJV).

Rebuke the mouths of those who try to tell you that your life will amount to nothing. Silence the voices, even in your own head, that seem to suggest that you are too messed up to be any good. Speak the Word of God over your life. If you are reading this chapter, in this book, it's because you are still alive. Regardless of what stage, age or phase of life you are in currently, God is not finished with you yet. His promises to you are yes and amen.

> For thus saith the Lord, that after seventy years be accomplished at Babylon I will visit you, and perform my good word toward you, in causing you to return to this place. For I know the thoughts that I think toward you, saith the Lord, thoughts of peace, and not of evil, to give you an expected end." (Jeremiah 29:10-11 KJV).

In the Book of Genesis, Joseph's own brothers plotted to kill him. They had thrown him in the pit. They sold him out. Yet at the end of his days, God's promises prevailed. God's plans will always be fulfilled. I have found in my own life that God is not the author of confusion. However, in all the chaos, He is still the God in control.

You are not too far gone. Your situation is nothing too hard for God to deliver you from. You must, however, stay in prayer and get guidance from the God of the Bible. I do not believe in jumping ship just because the waters are rough, but if you know in your heart of hearts that you have done all you can to salvage that marriage, to help that child, to do right by your boss, but whatever you do does not change the situation; there is no improvement or no intent to improve or appreciate, coming back to you from the other side, then maybe it's time to make that uncomfortable decision to evacuate. That evacuation might very well save your life. It did mine. It's time to release the seatbelts and get out.

My breaking point became my inflection point, and I am so grateful to God. Now my soul is free to prosper. I am able to soar to unlimited heights. Excited about what God will have me do. His love lifted me. His love will most certainly lift you as well. Now, He is extending His hands to you – hold it, trust it, lean into it. He is pulling you up. So get up—step up; I'll see you at the top.

My friend:

Arise, shine; for thy light is come, and the glory of the Lord is risen upon thee. (Isaiah 60:1 KJV)

ABOUT THE AUTHOR

Joanne delightfully joined the group of esteemed authors in contributing to *The Breaking Point*. She hopes that her chapter will bring the insight you need to find passion and purpose, so that you might live your best life now.

Speaker and author of *HIGHER ALTITUDES, Life Lessons Learnt at 35,000 feet*. Joanne Harte, is the Director of Christian Arts & Empowerment Network. She is the host of *The Midnight Run*, a live program aired on Facebook every second and fourth Saturday morning at 12 am. She is the co-host of *Kingdom Proclamations Live*, a program on FB each Saturday after lunch.

As a ghost writer, she writes and publishes non-fiction for first-time Christian authors, focusing on sharing their inspirational life stories. Once a week she can be found sharing a two minute encouragement message called "A Moment of Truth."

Joanne merges her faith in God and degrees in Religious Education and Christian Counseling with her life's experience, to empower women. With over thirty-five years in the airline industry, she has employed her expertise in hospitality and protocol to train ushers, greeters, volunteers and event staff for the local churches in the New York area.

She hails from Georgetown, Guyana, South America, and now resides in East Hartford, Connecticut with her family. She holds to the truth that Jesus was the best thing that ever happened to her. She can be reached via messenger on the Facebook page of Christian Arts and Empowerment Network. Her book, *HIGHER ALTITUDES, Life Lessons Learnt at 35,000 feet*, can be accessed on www.amazon.com/author/joanneharte.

12

GROWING THROUGH GRIEF

Nicole S. Thomas

Have you ever had an out-of-body experience? The kind where you feel like you are watching a movie in which you are the star, but you didn't write the movie, you're not directing the movie, and you have zero control over any aspect of the movie's content. That is how I felt after my husband died just two months after being diagnosed with stage 4 liver cancer leaving me all alone to raise our three young children. I was devastated. My love story had abruptly come to an end.

I have believed in the power of love for as long as I can remember. As a young girl, I dreamed of getting married. I dreamed of a big wedding. I would write out my wedding programs with detailed information on who would be in the wedding party, what songs would be sung, etc. I loved looking through bridal magazines, attending weddings. Cinderella was my favorite fairytale, and I was waiting for my Prince Charming to come rescue me from my abysmal life. However, I learned early in my dating life that "my" Prince Charming may not find me as quickly as Cinderella's found her.

I always dated with marriage in mind thinking to myself "this could be the one." Of course, I had my heart broken a few times in my teenage and young adult years while living in Texas and even after I moved to California with my grandparents. I began settling into my new life in California: going to school, working, and dating casually. I hadn't encountered a real love connection, but with each man I met, I still asked myself "could this be the one"? Again and again, a resounding "NO" was proven to be the answer. I was tired of meeting "Mr. Wrong" and decided just to let it go. I was done with dating! That was one of many breaking points in my life. I remember praying and asking God to send me someone who would love me for me and who would only have eyes for me.

In the meantime, I was reintroduced to friends of my aunties that lived down the street. I developed a great friendship with one of the young ladies. This friend visited me one day and was excited that her brother was coming home from prison. At that time, I had been in California a little over a year, but her brother had been in prison, and I had never met him. She was full of joy, and it was evident that she loved her brother and had missed him terribly. I was taken by surprise when she said, "You should meet him when he comes home. I think y'all would make a cute couple." I was puzzled as to why she thought it would be cute if I were coupled with someone who was getting out of prison. I knew he was her brother, but didn't the fact that he was getting out of prison mean that he had some issues, to say the least? Well...I was taught to be nice, so I simply smiled and said, "Really?"

As his release date neared, I began to hear more stories from his siblings and my family about the young man. The most surprising comments came from my grandfather when he said, "He is a good guy. He just got mixed in with the wrong crowd. I like him." I thought, "What? Wow!" That was the best thing I had ever heard my grandfather say about any of the young men in the neighborhood. I was intrigued, but the fact he was getting *out of prison* still weighed on my mind. A few weeks after he was released, my friend invited me to her home to meet him. He came onto their front porch trying to look tough, but a wide smile soon covered his face. He would later tell me when he learned I was a distant relative of my aunties from Texas, he assumed that *I* might be a little rough around the edges. He was pleasantly surprised as we began to talk and get to know each other.

We began dating, and it did not take long for us to become inseparable. It was a whirlwind romance. My Prince Charming had finally found me, and we were going to live happily ever after. I found him to be loving and attentive. We were both young and looking to improve ourselves. He helped me study for tests and do my homework. He held me accountable to my goals. I showed him the same support that he was showing me. I helped him look for jobs and establish some things for himself. We grew to become each other's greatest supporters. We moved in together, I became pregnant, we rededicated our lives to the Lord, and got married. All within a year and a half. My life began to progress, and I could hardly believe it. I had someone who loved me who was kind, sensitive to my needs, supportive, and family-oriented. I knew God had smiled on me.

We went on to build a life together rooted in our love for God and each other. He told me that he had prayed and asked God for a solid foundation while he was in prison. He believed that God sent me to begin that solid foundation. He was an awesome father to our three children and active in their care naturally, spiritually, and emotionally. I had never experienced a man taking such care and interest in his children. I am so blessed to have had a husband and father to my children that was as special as he was. We thought we would be together forever.

My husband was diagnosed with stage 4 cancer at the beginning of March, 2010. He was originally given six months to live. I was sure this diagnosis would turn into a testimony that he would live to tell; however, it did not work out that way. He only made it a couple of months until May 8, 2010. My heart was broken to say the least. I now had to figure out how to move forward without my partner and best friend and raise our three young children alone. I operated in survival mode for many years. My prayer was simply LORD, KEEP ME. I did not want to backslide, lose my mind, or make a decision that would catapult my life into a downward spiral. When my husband died, we were in ministry together, overseeing/pastoring a group of people in our home. I wasn't sure I could keep going in the direction we were headed together. I knew how people received me as a married woman, however, I wasn't sure how I would be received as a single woman in ministry. From my experience, "the church world" was not always supportive of single young women who were ministry leaders. I found myself in a pattern of trying to be what other leaders thought I should be. I was not processing my grief; I was running off adrenalin. Because all the weight of caring for my family and myself was on me, I did not want to make any more decisions. I did not want conflict. I just wanted to be kept! Kept from falling apart, kept from falling away, kept from falling out. However, it seemed everyone was expecting me to be the same person I was before my husband died. That was impossible, I was forever changed.

My husband's death was a true breaking point. I began to realize that grief was not as much about my husband's death as it was about the life I would now live without him in it. I had to learn that grief was not just about crying and being sad. But it is a process that is idiosyncratic to each person. I had to process the trauma and the grief of my husband's death to truly move forward. There was no way around it. After processing my grief, I realized it afforded me the opportunity to grow and help others. I help widows process the death of their husbands through a six-week course "Growing Through Grief." Participants follow the three-step healing framework, which focuses on Understanding Grief, Creating Space, and Managing Grief. The course provides live training, community, and accountability, which are essential for true healing to take place.

Perhaps my story has resonated with you? Are you a widow or do you know someone who is grieving but is having difficulty processing the death of their loved one? I would love to connect. Helping others has given purpose to my husband's death. Now, I truly know the truth of Romans 8:28 (KJV). "And we know that all things work together for good to them that love God, to them who are the called according to his purpose."

ABOUT THE AUTHOR

Nicole S. Thomas is co-author of the book, *The Breaking Point*, which is scheduled for release in April 2022.

Nicole is a minister, Christian counselor, and grief coach. She seeks to spread the love of God while encouraging and equipping those seeking healing and wholeness. Nicole has learned invaluable lessons on the importance of keeping God as her anchor while prioritizing and maintaining life/work balance.

A philanthropist and volunteer in her community, Nicole has served as a member of the board of directors of several nonprofit organizations. In 2017, she expanded her work and influence in the community by establishing Providence Institute & Resource Center.

A woman of strength and resilience, Nicole has overcome

many challenges that helped shape her into the genuine encourager and person of courage that she is today. She is the mother of three children Christolenae, Christopher, and NiCade that epitomize God's gift of strength, determination, and unconditional love. After becoming a widow, Nicole created a Facebook group in support of others who have lost their soulmate. In an effort to continue supporting widows, she also recently launched a six-week course "Growing through Grief."

Connect with Nicole

- email: info@providenceirc.org
- website: www.providenceirc.org
- Facebook: @ProvidenceIRCN4P or Nicole Thomas
- Instagram: ProvidenceIRCN4P or nicki_live_laugh_love

13

UNDEFEATED

Marilyn Evans

I thought that because she birthed me, we would have a bond. I always felt like she hated me because of the attachment I had to my daddy. A mother isn't supposed to inflict physical harm on her children, however, this wasn't the case for me. The burn on my shoulder from the hot comb while pressing my hair was a reminder of how she felt towards me. Her beating me with a wire hanger, because I refused to give her the money my daddy left for me when he died.

It all began to take a toll on me. I was done with trying to please those who're supposed to love me, protect me, and nurture me. The bullying had to stop. The verbal and physical abuse had to stop. I never thought I would feel this way toward my own mother, but I got tired, and I was at my breaking point.

What got me to my breaking point with my mom was my physical and mental health. I had neglected myself for so long that my health was failing and weight was out of control. When I went to the doctor, and they said, "Ms. Evans, you are prediabetic, and we are sending you to prediabetic counseling." I knew that was bad. I don't like needles or blood and the nurse showed me how to prick my finger. Shaking like a crackhead trying to prick my finger, I made up in my mind, I needed two things: counseling and coming face to face that I hadn't truly forgiven my mom.

I have been in counseling since 2013. I was holding on to the unforgiveness. I was waiting on an apology from her for everything that had happened to me. I never received the apology from my mom. I had to learn to release it and truly give it to God because He was the only one that could deliver me and set me free from the demons of unforgiveness.

But then I had a breakthrough. A female pastor told me, "Marilyn, you have to release it. You have to release it verbally by saying every person's name who has hurt you. We prayed together, and I did exactly that. The miracles and the peace that come when you become obedient to God's Word.

Now, when I talk to my mom, I can tell the difference. My relationship with her is not what it used to be. She is the only living parent I have on this earth. I love my mom and know everything I have been through was supposed to happen, because that pain birthed my purpose. "And be ye kind one to another, tender hearted, forgiving one another, even as God for Christ's sake haith forgiven you" (Ephesians 4:32 KJV).

We get lost in our families and daily lives. We forget the foundation on which we stand. I had to learn that you put no one before God. I was sacrificing myself and God by putting everyone before Him. When I changed the roles, God first, I could see what God had for me.

I could see the path He had designed just for me. I could see my blessing and could hear God's voice clear. I thanked God for my purpose. It was not easy. It was extremely painful and exhausting. I also had to realize that God forgives us of our sins daily. Who am I not to forgive my mom. I had to forgive my mom, not only in my mind but in my heart.

When I finally released the unforgiveness and the pain, my healing was birthed. My blessings, peace, and purpose, I can see it. It took faith and obedience to hear God's voice. "You can be healed. You can forgive, because it's not for the person who hurt you, it's for you."

Break those words in shackles. Take your power back. Release it by screaming or crying or on your knees talking to God. Open your heart to receive what He has for you. Your Breaking Point is now. "And when ye stand praying, forgive, if ye have ought against any: that your Father also which is in heaven may forgive you your trespasses" (Mark 11:25 KJV).

ABOUT THE AUTHOR

Marilyn Evans is an inspiring motivational speaker for mental health, healing, and forgiveness. Her first book, *"When the Little Girl Is Healed, The Woman Will Show Up,"* explains the journey she unwittingly took to become the woman she is today. Marilyn carefully steps through the path from abuse, depression, and anger, into the role of the powerful, accomplished business owner of today. She published her book in August of 2021. Her nieces, nephews, and godchildren motivate her to be the best she can be.

Marilyn was born in Montgomery, Alabama. She graduated from high school in 1994 and went on to earn her Associate Degree in Computer Information Systems from John Patterson Technical College in 1999. She remained in her hometown until she decided to join the

United States Air Force in San Antonio, Texas. Marilyn returned to Alabama and has been in her current role of City Letter Carrier for the United States Postal Service for 18 years.

Marilyn is joining forces as a co-author in *The Breaking Point*. In this new book, she will share how to trust the process to move past the breaking points in your life. We all have them. She encourages her readers to go through the pain and into their purpose.

Connect with Marilyn

- Instagram: Marilyn.Evans1
- Facebook: Marilyn Evans
- Website: Marilynevansenterprises.com
- Email: meenterprises75@gmail.com
- Twitter: @Marilyn5925

14

I QUIT

Shannon Hancock

Do not let the world make you hard. That is what kept running through my head as I pondered how to manage the situation. How was I going to do it? Do I stay or do I go? What would I say or how?

Would I tell them? My back was against the wall in my decision because so many people would be affected. This one little turn of events could impact so many people. I was fed up and done! I wanted out as soon as possible, but how was I going to do that? It was a warm summer morning when the phone rang. I was sitting at the table eating a bowl of cereal as the light from the morning sun was beaming through the windows. This was the call I had been waiting for, and I knew my prayers were answered. I had struggled for weeks to keep my composure at work and knew this would be the right direction for my path. Having endured so much stress and pain from this reoccurring situation that I was not sure which direction my path would take with a new adventure. But I knew I was at my breaking point. I wanted so much more in life and for myself and my children. As a single mom, I knew my decision could impact and test my ability to continue to put food on the table for my sons. I was at the lowest point in my life. I had just lost my job of six years. My company filed bankruptcy, and I knew I needed a new career path. I couldn't help but wonder, was this job where I was supposed to be or was there more out there for me? I wanted something different. I wanted a way out.

After I lost my job, I took a new job as a sales supervisor. I was excited. I loved sales, and I loved people. What a perfect match! Soon after taking the new job, I realized that it was a great fit for me to continue to develop a new team and help the company make money. I wanted to have a positive influence in their lives. And of course, starting at a new company, I wanted to make a good name for myself. I was happy in my new role, and most importantly, excited to go to work each day. Yes, the shift was not the greatest, but I knew once I hit the sales floor the sky was the limit. As a genuine *people person*, I quickly made friends with my coworkers and fellow sales supervisors. We had a small group, so I felt confident that I could make a significant impact.

I later discovered this would be a huge mistake. How

could my judgment be so wrong in the beginning? I thought with having a small group that it would be pretty tight knit. It was at the start, but not as tight as what I was used to. I felt like an outsider within a few weeks of taking this new job. I didn't know anybody in my area, so I had no one to raise my concerns to. I asked myself, "Was this normal? Did they always treat everybody like this, or was it just me?" Because I came from the outside and quickly made myself a name on the sales floor, I felt neglected from the team. I had 39 employees who were on my team, 39 at-home agents I had to communicate with. Daily-set sales, goals, writing reviews, I continued supporting the team I felt wasn't supporting me. At this point, I truly felt like this is not the place I needed to be.

However, I needed to provide for my children. I was always taught to *suck it up* and *fake it till you make it*, which has continued to be my motto in life. I was bullied and talked down to by other sales supervisors. How could this be? This was my team; this is the close-knit group that I wanted and felt comfortable being close to. I wanted out. I knew that this was not normal. I wanted to take my energy to hold another level with this new company, but how could I turn back and look at the people who were supposed to support me but were talking down to me every single day. Being bullied by my peers, it did not feel like I had a choice but to decide to walk away. I had a terrific opportunity looking at me straight in the face.

With a phone call I received this morning, will this be my way out?

After multiple phone calls and job interview, I knew I got a new job, but I set my plan into place of how I was going to get out of the job I was in. At that point the only way I could figure of getting out of my current job was to just walk out. This is something new for me. I have never quit a job this way, nor had I ever thought I would ever be in this situation. Too many times, I knew I would go home and cry after my shift because I'd never felt so low, and I had never felt that my peers accepted me for who I was. So many thoughts running through my head of how I was going to break this to my team or was I going to bring it to my team? I was worried it would just be lonely and uneventful, in the sense I was there one day and gone the next. Lives were going to be affected, but I knew that my life was much more than that. I felt that I had to be present in my life and made sure that I was this stronger person that I saw myself becoming. After I got the green light in my offer letter from the new company, I set my plan in action; I got up and went to work like normal once I went through security. I made my way to the desk, and I proceeded to gather my personal items, quickly and discreetly trying to figure out the best plan of action to tell them I was leaving. After the first person glared at me, I decided to implement my plan of action. I asked one of my fellow employees to walk me to security so I could hand in my badge. I was done, I was really done, and I felt like a ton of bricks was lifted off my shoulders. As I walked out the door for the final time, I realized it was still early in the evening. I could still go have dinner with my children. Leaving there that night I would not be the same person, but I knew I was a better person. I felt so much relief that night as I was walking to my car. I knew I was supposed to start my new job in just a few days, a job I felt that I would find to absolutely love. I felt very welcomed the first day I walked in. I knew from the start that this was it, that this was my calling. I knew this was where I was supposed to be, and I knew from day one that I was loved by the staff. For the next six years I walked through the doors of that company, and I loved every day of it.

The things I found out about myself were that I was worthy of anything and everything I ever wanted including my dream job, and I found out that I never want to feel stuck; my life and my children were worth more. Can you relate to my story? Have you ever been in a position where you felt that you wanted to give up and walk away? Just know we all have a breaking point in life, but you can strive everyday to make it your best day!

ABOUT THE AUTHOR

There is nothing more powerful than the bold clarity of the human voice. Living in a society masked often as a war zone, it takes advocates, born with the courage to use their voices; in order to see meaningful progression , on our journey toward a better world. Leading by effortless example, is the energized professional, Shannon Hancock.

Shannon Hancock is an author, motivational speaker, organizational guru, and CEO and Founder of Shannon Hancock, LLC; a specialty centered around the formation of finding practical solutions, through the simplistic principles of cleaning, assortment, and organization; in order to foster space for positive thinking and personal clarity in the lives of her clients. Shannon's effervescent nature has reputed her as one of the best in the professional arena, as she is often called upon to aid in diverse leadership roles; including having been a customs broker for Amazon, and as a production manager for The Kim Jacobs Show.

Shannon's mantra is simple: she believes in the good of all people; especially women. She anthems that with a strong soul and support from all sisters, we can take over the world; one person at a time.

Shannon has a premier vernacular concerning women's issues, and often relies on the strength of her experience as a single mother and divorcee; as rudders helping to steer other women on their journey toward healing and the inner solace needed, to find their personal and professional voices.

When Shannon is not out advocating for the causes of women, she is a beloved member of her local professional community, and the proud mother of two sons, Tyler and Tanner.

Shannon Hancock. Leader. Speaker. Women's Enthusiast.

Connect with Shannon

- Email: shannon694@gmail.com

15

SURVIVING POST-PARTUM DEPRESSION

Ilesha Carney

Being a parent isn't easy and being a boy mom is even more difficult in my opinion. There I was, pregnant with my second child. What should have been one of the most exciting times in my life was the most stressful. I was scared and uncertain about many things when one sunny morning in October, baby number two arrived!

I'd like to recount how easy or difficult the labor was, but truthfully, I can't. I have total amnesia from the arrival to the hospital until we returned home days later. Most mothers cherish the moments they have bonding with their newborn. Like holding them for the first time. I didn't have that, and perhaps this is where the disconnect began. Nights were long and hard. I was attempting to breastfeed for the first time, but it wasn't working. He would often fall asleep without eating much. If he wanted to sleep all day, I'd let him because I wanted to sleep too. During a routine wellness visit, the baby was said to be underweight. They took him immediately by ambulance to the hospital.

My anxiety was at an all-time high, and I felt awful. Not being a new mom, I should have known better, right? The hospital staff allowed me to stay in the room with the baby. They watched me like a hawk. The staff even alluded to me not having the means to feed him and was perhaps watering down his bottles to make them stretch. This was actually my first attempt at breastfeeding, and since he wasn't latching on well, this was a huge source of frustration for me. So if he wasn't crying to eat, I didn't force it. The nurses told me to give up and strictly bottle feed. To see my breast fill with milk every day was a constant reminder that I was failing as a mom. After three days in the hospital, he was alert, bottle feeding well and discharged.

Once we returned home, I still didn't interact with the baby much. The love was there, but it was difficult to focus on his needs. I wanted to sleep a lot. Dark drapes hung over all the windows in the house and remained closed all day, rarely getting out of bed unless it was to eat. Always tearful, I began to eat my feelings. Oddly enough, food was the only thing that brought me joy. Phone calls went unanswered and attending social gatherings became less frequent. Withdrawal from family and friends was common. The rapid weight gain made me even more tired, miserable and uncomfortable with my appearance. I had no desire to cook, clean or groom myself. Often feeling exhausted and stressed, I was also very short-tempered and unaffectionate with my children. When I felt down and wanted to cry, I did so in private. I never wanted my children to perceive me as weak because of course, I was a strong black woman, independent and could carry the weight of the world on my shoulders. We parents are so busy tending to everyone else that we often neglect our own physical and mental health. We've been conditioned to be strong and stoic. The glue that holds the family together. Well, during my postpartum check-up my doctor asked a series of questions that I answered very candidly. I could no longer pretend. This shell of a woman wasn't as strong as she appeared and had to surrender for the sake of her sanity and her children. The stigma of mental health in the black community often leads to undiagnosed illnesses and exacerbation of symptoms. This was true for me. This was the face of postpartum depression.

To understand this a little better, during pregnancy and after, a woman's hormones go haywire. This is believed to be one of the causes of postpartum depression. Surprisingly, young fathers struggle with this too. The stress of juggling home, work and the financial responsibilities of a new baby may be contributing factors. Short-lived symptoms are referred to as the baby blues, but long-term symptoms may actually be depression. The hormonal changes definitely affected my mood. My symptoms were common and included feelings of hopelessness, anxiety, guilt, excessive eating, weight gain, irritability and fatigue. Other symptoms can include forgetfulness, loss of interest in activities you once enjoyed, weight loss, and even thoughts of death or suicide.

Symptoms of overeating led me to gain 15 pounds after childbirth, although I still had 15 pounds left to shed from the weight I gained during pregnancy. I was told that my rapid weight gain was the cause of other problems I was experiencing and was eventually diagnosed with pseudo tumor cerebri. My body was producing an excessive amount of brain and spinal fluid and the symptoms mimicked that of a brain tumor. Being misdiagnosed several times and having my symptoms simply disregarded, was another source of stress for me. As my health continued to decline, my loved ones began to show concern for me following many unanswered calls and voicemails and my lack of participation in group events. I knew I needed to make a drastic change, but didn't know how. Being home all day with the children and having little interaction with the outside world wasn't helpful. I quit my job during my pregnancy and remained unemployed for months after. There was no desire to work. I was disconnected and out of touch. I realized that I was going nowhere fast and yearned to have a sense of normalcy. I was suffering, and so were my children. I'd reached my breaking point. Not wanting to take anti-depressants, I decided to try other coping methods first. Some suggestions were deep breathing, meditation, staying active, accepting help from family and friends, a change in routine and self-care. Some other treatments included counseling, medication, avoiding alcohol or Psychotherapy. Starting with small changes such as pulling back the drapes in the morning to let the sunshine in was helpful. Although I was still exhausted, I began to get dressed and comb my hair every single day. Eventually, I was able to get enough energy to go outside and began walking. It felt good to be in the sun. Sunlight helps increase serotonin levels. Serotonin is a hormone that helps stabilize our mood. Although these changes were great, it wasn't enough. Wanting to take more control over my life and career, I felt ready to return to work. This was a way to force myself into social interactions and establish a new routine. I was hired on with the first job to which I applied. I was still anxious and considered turning it down, but didn't. I showed up for work every day. Seeing how far I had come was amazing. Sometimes you have no idea how bad things are until you come out the other side. The dark cloud over my life was dissipating and alas, the breakthrough had come. I promoted quickly on the job, gained some new skills and made a transition within the medical field. I slowly started to return to normal. The bond with my children was strong, and my physical health was improving. My anxiety was gone, my thoughts were clear. I was feeling proud and accomplished instead of lazy and ineffective. I started to regain my confidence and it showed in my day-to-day life. I was finally on the mend and determined to gain victory over my illness.

Currently, my son is a healthy, lovable young man who's doing well. Through it all I learned that in order to be a good mom, I had to put myself first. Before being a mother, wife, sister or friend, I am a human being first. Someone with feelings, wants and needs that must be addressed in order for me to be my best self. For those suffering with postpartum depression, please know there is nothing abnormal about you. Many suffer from this, and you are not alone in your struggle. I encourage others to be unafraid and unashamed when it comes to asking for help. As seen with me, there can be some implicit biases and healthcare disparities surrounding women of color, but please don't let this be a deterrent. Anyone caring for a loved one during the postpartum period should familiarize themselves with the signs and symptoms of postpartum depression. Think about that one friend who's strong and seems to have it all together and is the "go to" person for everyone. When does she ever get the opportunity to be vulnerable? Check on her and reciprocate the support. The person going through it may not recognize the changes within themselves because they are too preoccupied with the challenges of life. Today I feel complete and whole. I give myself permission to be vulnerable, make mistakes and just be perfectly imperfect. Does any of this resonate with you? If so, please seek help now. It's always darkest before dawn but your breakthrough is coming.

ABOUT THE AUTHOR

Ilesha Carney is a debut author sharing her thoughts on postpartum depression in her first book, The Breaking Point. As a co-author, she hopes her words will provide knowledge and comfort to those who suffer from its effects long after childbirth. She is also in the process of writing a children's book

Working in the medical field for more than twenty years, Ilesha has been a licensed nurse for eleven years. She is currently a nurse supervisor for the largest Independent Physicians Association (IPA) in Northern California, where she has worked for nine years. A clinical educator, she has taught pharmacy technicians for seven years for Boston Reed College.

She has a keen eye for all things fashion and brings her

feminine energy into all things of beauty, poise, and style. Actively designing a beauty industry company, she'll introduce her unique line of self-care products to make women look and feel pretty from the inside out.

Ilesha is a "boy mom" to five handsome sons. She and her family have lived in Sacramento, California the past twenty years. Ilesha's friends have nicknamed her "Diva. Ilesha spends her free time with family and friends and enjoys listening to live music, jogging, and traveling.

Connect with Ilesha

- ixctheauthor@gmail.com.

16

CUTTING LOOSE: I CHOOSE ME

Sonja Babino

"I'm leaving and taking our sons with me."

He said absolutely nothing as I made this declaration. I write my story to the many women who have reached their breaking point in unhealthy relationships and need to walk away to save themselves. For seventeen years, I loved him and for seventeen years he hated me. At least it felt like hate. Being a woman of God I knew with everything in me this feeling would only be temporary. But what do you do when the man you love doesn't love you back? This was the question I had to ask myself repeatedly. Before I walked to the front room to inform him of my intentions, I looked at myself in the bathroom mirror, dried my eyes, and said "Today, I choose me."

Our sons knew only of our union, but through watching, they began to learn how toxic our union had become. For several years they watched me work long hours and sometimes thousands of miles away from home just to ensure we kept a roof over our heads, food in the refrigerator, and a vehicle in our driveway. I suffered silently without noticing that areas of my life were being affected negatively. My relationships with my friends suffered, the reconciliation with my own mother was not allowed and I began to make decisions on my job that would ultimately affect my job stability just to keep my family afloat. I remember thinking, God this isn't what you ordered for my life, it just can't be. The last straw was my health began to fail. I couldn't understand why I'd wake up more tired than when I went to sleep the night before. At night, my husband would randomly slam his hand on the mattress, and it would startle me awake. I began going to bed not able to sleep because I feared he would startle me. He wouldn't communicate to explain why because months prior he stopped talking to me. This was not new because throughout our marriage he'd often go silent for weeks without warning. These things began to wear on me both mentally and physically. I needed to evaluate the cost of me accepting such treatment. What my children were watching could easily become the blueprint for them as young men and that I simply could not have. With that I'd reached my breaking point.

I prayed fervently asking God to release me from marriage only if it were His will. My view of my spouse changed, and our relationship had grown to be unhealthy. I tried one last time to talk to him and said, "I know we've reached a place where we now function as two individuals living two separate lives. If your presence here is only for the sake of our sons and you no longer love me, tell me. But if you love me, tell me and I'll do whatever I need to do to make this work." I also pleaded with him to take care of his own health, as he'd been diagnosed years before with diabetes but refused to follow his physician's instructions. His health was failing, and it threatened his ability to be there for his sons in the future. "If for no one else, could you take care of your health so you can be there for your sons, I asked. He sat there on the edge of our bed staring at the floor and said nothing. He'd seemingly given up on us as a couple and as a father.

What good was I, giving all of me to someone who wouldn't bat an eye at meeting any of my spiritual, emotional, or physical needs? I'd become a shell of myself, no longer able to take care of me. The empty feeling at the pit of my stomach became my norm, and it took all the strength I had to not cry in front of my children. I saved those tears to rock myself to sleep many of nights. I took some time away to talk to God and seek clarity. While praying for clarity in my decision-making, that is when my heart was opened, and I surrendered to His guidance.

God revealed that I'd been waiting seventeen years for someone other than myself to love me when it should've been me loving me all along. I then chose myself. This decision didn't come easy.

In the church I'd learned the value of marriage and that it should last a lifetime. I stayed because of my loose interpretation of the covenant and the criteria by which it could be dissolved, infidelity, that we did not meet. This covenant was only being held by half of our union. But what God revealed to me in my time of prayer and supplication was that we weren't equally yoked. My faith sustained me, and his lack of faith drained me and quite frankly wouldn't allow us to move forward. Like two oxen at odds with one another, we simply could not perform the task God set before us.

There were three mind shifts that took place to get me to the place of resolution. The first was choosing myself and not limiting my thinking to either/or. It was not as simple as I could either stay or leave. I could have stayed hoping for my spouse's desire to change, meanwhile losing myself in the waiting. This choice, however, would have been to the detriment of my sons who are future husbands and fathers. That would not have been the example of love and fidelity I wanted them to have. I had to decide what was the most loving thing to do. The second was to honor myself. By showing up for myself and God, I felt His love pouring though my broken heart. I started to take care of my body by first saying no to the harmful relationship that was my marriage and making my way back to worship that allowed me to heal my spiritual wounds. Thirdly, I realized how much I had been hiding from living fully. In marriage I'd given up on myself and the dreams of reconciliation with my mother when all the while he maintained a very close relationship with his very own. When I removed the conditions from my life that were placed on me by my spouse, I realized I could live fully. I became courageous instead of thinking that life was over for me or that it was too late to be happy after many years. I'd become comfortable in my discomfort.

If you are hiding in your comfort zone, or you think that God has given up on you and placed you in a toxic place to die, it's time to recalibrate your faith. Learn to check in with God's desires for you by seeking Him in prayer. It's hard and it will be scary because you struggle in hearing what you want to hear when seeking His advice. Make a personal commitment to love and trust yourself again. This won't fail you even if you think it seems your choice might hurt another. Imagine if I'd stayed because of the optics to the outside world, meanwhile sacrificing myself. My children would've suffered ultimately, and my sacrifice was for them. Tune in with your body. Your body has a way of either feeling light or constricted and heavy as a reaction to the people, situations, and things around you.

In my previous marriage, in the times I wanted it to work so badly, my body felt sick, my stomach queasy and I was restless. Even in the times I thought things were okay, I was uneasy and anxious about the other shoe that would ultimately drop. In toxic friendships, a heaviness presents in my chest alarming me to existing resentment and the need to set boundaries for myself. However, music, on the other hand, makes my whole heart and body smile. Those were the ques for me, and they may present differently for you. The message here is to simply listen to God's voice and your body. You'll experience a deep peace and a knowing that you will never want to leave. So please, choose yourself, take care of self and understand yourself. You will be able to take care of those who depend on you.

ABOUT THE AUTHOR

Non-fiction author Sonja Babino has recently contributed to an anthology, The Breaking Point releasing in April, 2022.

With five published works, Sonja has a uniquely wry voice that shines through in her latest work comprised of various online dating stories. She has spent a lifetime writing down her thoughts and sharing humorous experiences with those close to her. It is her unique storytelling that captivates readers.

Her chosen career is as an I.T. Professional.

Sonja is committed to using her life as an example to women and men alike to show that you don't have to look like what you've been through in hopes that they, too, would be inspired to push through.

Connect with Sonja

- Linkedin: https://www.linkedin.com/in/sonja-garrett-5238761
- Website: www.sonjababino.com
- Email: sonjababino@yahoo.com
- Facebook: https://www.facebook.com/sonja.babino/
- Instagram:SonjaGarrett247

17

THE SWITCH UP

Lissha Sadler

"And he said unto me, My grace is sufficient for thee: for my strength is made perfect in weakness.Most gladly, therefore, will I rather glory in my infirmities, that the power of Christ may rest upon me.Therefore I take pleasure in infirmities, in reproaches, in necessities, in persecutions, in distresses for Christ's sake: for when I am weak, then am I strong" (2 Corinthians 12:9–10 KJV).

As a radio host, I always talk about a Go Moment. A Go Moment is when our thoughts and execution come together. We are so mindful of how we pour into others, but when we speak to ourselves, most of the time, we speak in lack and fear, talking ourselves out of the moves and ideas placed in our spirit. But what happens when we don't execute? I believe God will allow a change so intense to manifest in our lives that pressure is applied.

This process is what I call the Switch up, and it often occurs at different points in our life. At this moment, for me, it was my divorce.

Most little girls fantasize about being wives and mothers. The "white picket fence" is a little girl's dream, because it represents the idea of love, security, and happiness. Growing up in a Baptist family,where marriage was always instilled to be a forever thing, even though divorce happened every day. So, for me, failure was not an option. But I wasn't paying attention and lost sight that the marital vehicle was already dismantled and sitting on bricks for some time. We had stopped being present. I say WE because you are two people who should be walking as one. So if one fails, you both fail, and the marriage dies.

Many of our experiences in life determine a lot of our choices, which often change the order that love, marriage, and babies come. See, I've learned that when I venture off and make choices that lack God and intent, I always seem to end up in a self-inflicted "trick bag." Which turned out to be my marriage and divorce, with a process that was stressful and full of emotionally self-inflicted traumatizing ups and downs.

Honestly, I felt abandoned until I saw Pastor Sarah Jakes Roberts' "Apply Pressure" sermon on YouTube. Her words resonated with me because I saw my life being played out. She was delivering a message. Listening to her this day, I had my *ah–ha* moment. I lived life, but I stopped trusting God's plan and started believing in my own plan, which caused Him to Switch Up on me. "The Switch Up," I can tell you is not a course of action we take voluntarily. I believe God has had to step in and force your movement, a divine shift. It can be minor or significant, but it is a change that is a necessity for you to fulfill the plan He has for you.

Growing up, I considered divorce a form of failure unless the situation was unhealthy. I now understand that I made an unrealistic assumption about marriage and divorce, because I lacked critical facts. Marriage is not a trend or a thing to do. It has the power to build and destroy if you are not with the right person. And divorce is not a bad thing; it prevents you from continuing on a dead-end road to nowhere. Sometimes the most profound truths come from difficult situations and uncomfortable experiences.

When my husband told me he was filing for divorce, all I could say was, "Okay!" That was the only word that could leave my lips. My mind turned off at that moment, and I believe that was God's way of telling me to shut up to prevent any further conversations or questions. There was no need. People have to do what is best for them, and everyone you meet is not meant to be in your life forever. Everything will always work out in your favor.

Learning to trust the process won't feel good when you're in it because you cannot control events.

Instantly, Sarah Jakes Roberts' sermon was on repeat in my mind, "God broke the covenant with your ex. You couldn't walk away from the relationship, so God made the relationship walk away from you. And you might have been asking God why He let that happen to you. God says to tell you that you were going to settle for something less than you, so He had to set you free."

Before I got married, I was in a secure spot. Now, I had become less independent and more dependent, so I was not prepared. One thing I knew was that this was all part of His plan, and honestly, panic seeped in, briefly taking over my mind. All I could think was, "What am I going to do?." My footing was shaky, I was in a house, not working full time, and my son had just started college. It caused panic in my mind, but not in my soul. The problem was I could not see what lie ahead. My vision was temporarily blocked.

My steps were always ordered, so I should have found peace and security, knowing God wouldn't leave me now. But being human, I didn't, not entirely. The problem was me, because I was not the controller of my life, and He was showing me. All He needed was for me to let go and let Him have free reign. I was in a spiritual fight for control between myself and God. Even in the foolish moment of anxiety and panic, my soul was always at peace. All I had to do was be still because I had nothing to worry about moving forward. Don't get me wrong, giving God complete control is not easy or instant. It is a scary thing to do. You feel like you're walking on a dark path, only able to see one set of footprints at a time.

Everything seemed to be coming at me all at once. I was so unfocused I didn't see anything but total darkness. I intended to trust God and let Him have His way, but enlightenment didn't last long. Being human and emotional, we tend to trip over our own feet, and trusting Him becomes secondary to our thoughts and feelings. I was giving Him control, but only when convenient for me, and that is not how faith works. Faith only works if you can completely trust and accept God's will. Yes, it can be uncomfortable, but God must execute His divine shift in your life to take you to the next level.

I allowed myself to panic yet again, because not only was I dealing with a horrible divorce process, and move in sixty days, but I now had to add surgery to the list. I had no plan of action in place. Everything I could think of had failed or was delayed. Feeling defeated, I had surgery with little to no healing time, because I had to finish packing up the house. I felt abandoned at that moment, but by who? By myself, I failed to protect myself fully. Remember when I said, "Sometimes the deepest truths come from the most difficult situations and uncomfortable experiences." Well, this moment in time was my breaking point, and I did the only thing I could once the house was sold. I stayed in a hotel until my next move was revealed. I was tired of fighting a losing battle. The week after my surrender, I had a full-time job with full benefits.

I now understand why God was telling me to let go. I wasn't listening, so He had to show me. He allowed things to get out of order in my life until I stopped fighting Him. When I finally did, it was like everything fell into place, although delayed four months. Two weeks after I started working, I was approved for an apartment. God made me whole despite me being in the way. I learned a hard lesson about moving in life by faith.

Trusting the process is most important because it never goes well when you fight with God to have control. We have to stop having faith when life looks safe and start trusting Him when things are at their worst. People can't make you whole, but God can. When you give unto the Lord, He will provide you with more. Pressed down and shaken together, all blessings running over. Your shift will be gradual. God has given you grace and mercy already. Now you have to give it to yourself and stop fighting His will. Give Him complete control so He can position and protect you. The more you stay in control, the weaker you become, and the more challenging and traumatic your Switch Up will be.

ABOUT THE AUTHOR

Lissha Sadler is a co-author of *The Breaking Point.*

Lissha is called the "Literary Plug" by many of her clients. As CEO of Intriguing Moves Inc—her umbrella company for Intriguing Moves PR, Divaz Lit, and Intriguing Pens Publications—Lissha loves to experience client's passion for their craft. She is a social media manager, author advocate, literary consultant, avid reader, contributing writer, and now, author.

In addition to her literary accomplishments, Lissha is a producer and co-host on the uber-popular podcast, Let's Chat w/ Mz Toni and Lissha. A two-time award-winning show, Let's Chat hit the airways on October 26, 2013 when two avid readers talked about literature and life.

That conversation birthed a space that became a cocoon for both aspiring and veteran authors to showcase their literary talents and connect with their readers.

Lissha is also the head writer of "Hardcore Grind," her column of great interviews that appear in four print and online magazines.

Despite her numerous accolades, Lissha's most significant accomplishment is her launch of the Visions and Books Literary Expo, now in its third year. The expo is near and dear to Lissha as she wanted to create a space for readers, to bless them with a "31 Flavors Reading Experience" and give back to the community simultaneously.

Lissha is looking forward to adding her new, creative, and diverse voice to the literary world. Keep up with Lissha's movements by following her robust social media accounts.

Connect with Lissha

- Facebook @Lissha Sadler
- Instagram @LisshaSadler @Lets_chat_radio
- Twitter @Lisssha; TikTok @LisshaSadler

18

DISCOVERING MY STRENGTH

Carolyn Coleman

"*Being confident of this very thing that he which hath begun a good work in you will perform it until the day of Jesus Christ*" (Philippians 1:6 KJV).

I was done with the party life that didn't satisfy me anymore. I had enough of being second to his friends and done with feeling unappreciated. I had put everyone before my wants and desires, and dreams. Now, I was done with feeling like I was wasting my life and not accomplishing something I could be proud of. Enough of going through life unfulfilled and empty, catering to others. But what do I do? How will I survive? I have a child, no job and my husband wants a divorce. Help me, Jesus. I don't know what to do?

Have you been there? Have you gone through something so devastating it forced you to dig deep within and pull on strength you didn't even know you had? I did. It forced me to learn to focus, to place blinders on and move at my pace. Being stubborn can be an attribute; it can create resilience.

My mind was all over the place; life as I knew it was about to change. Not wanting to move. Not knowing what to do next. Getting up meant moving. I did not want to talk to anyone. Talking meant explaining, answering questions. That is not who I am. Sometimes you have to reconcile some things within yourself before you can communicate with others. Just because you are comfortable with a situation does not mean that is where you belong. It can sometimes mean you are settling. Why should I settle? Newness brings anxiety. I wondered why I had these feelings, because I had detached long before he spoke those words. One thing for sure, I knew moving forward I had to find my strength and my worth. Work is therapeutic for me. It gives me purpose. Having a degree of structure keeps me balanced. Knowing someone depends on you gives you a reason to move forward. You have to create a new and better life for you and your family.

I have not accomplished my dreams. Dreams of becoming a therapist; all I needed to do was finish the program. I wanted to have a career; to accomplish this would fill a void. It would not take all of my problems away, but at least I would have it.

I was excited when I received my acceptance letter into the therapy program. Ready to get started on this career path, I was there on time. After orientation, it just did not feel right. I just walked away from the offer of a lifetime. It just did not click for me. I summed it up, everything is not for everyone.

Later, I realized it was a much stronger force. Who knew this was God's way of pulling me away from this and steering me into my rightful path?

Unsure how I heard about the nursing program, but I applied.

It was a one year program. We had a very eclectic group. Young, mature Black, White, empty nesters. It was a structured program; these were the people we would get to know WELL. We were going to travel this path together.

Using the stethoscope for the first time was magical. I actually heard breath sounds and heart tones. Mastering taking blood pressures was scary but fulfilling. Palpating pulses and practicing on each other was encouraging.

I was enjoying learning nursing practices, the human body and how to treat patients with their various disease processes. When asked what would I do next? I did not hesitate. Get my bachelor's degree in nursing.

I kept school and work in the correct order. After all mandatory classes had been completed, I was accepted into the nursing program. Now this will separate the women from the girls. Nursing school is no joke.

You have to take a brief moment for yourself to clear your head. My child's field trips helped. It was our time together, some time for me to forget about work and classes for just a little while. The kids are so carefree, jumping and running. Life is grand for them; not a care in the world.

No matter how smart you think you are, you have to study harder. You can only fail two classes. And if that happens, you are out. Nursing just clicked with me. No prior experience, I had never been exposed to anyone sick. I had to study. Not just study, but retain this information and write a flawless paper and pass the exam in order to pass this class. Yet to fail a class, I was not going to fail this one. Lord, thank you for favor and protection. Not attending class: not an option. I had to find my strength. School was more important. There is a great deal of sacrifices made with nursing school. Limited social life, if any, especially if you are taking this seriously. My final class was bizarre. Nothing pleased my instructor; she scored me low enough to pass. The more frustrated with her, the harder I worked. Discipline became a friend. I can have a sharp tongue, but I stayed the course and kept my mouth closed. I just needed to pass. And pass I did.

Praise God.

Graduation day was here. Family and friends were by my side, as usual, to support me. As I received my diploma and went back to my seat, I sat there and breathed in and out. Smiled and started giggling. "It is mine, and they cannot take it back." The guy sitting next to me looked, laughed and agreed. "No, they cannot."

Who would have ever thought this would be me? You are seeing people in their most vulnerable moments and telling them, "It is fine. I will keep you protected." We leave dignity at the door, and we laugh, shake our heads and proceed.

What do you like about nursing? I am often asked. Seeing the process work, people who are sick getting well. People who are transitioning from life to death. You can be their comfort along with assisting their family with their grieving. Just by allowing them to express themselves and to let them know you care. It is hard emotionally, especially unexpected death, but you, as the healthcare professional, have to take the lead and cry another day.

The human body is fascinating, how it tries to repair

itself. How strong it is. People do not often appreciate the marvel of their bodies. The abuse they put it through. And when it finally fails, they look to us—the nurse—to patch it back together. How many times have I heard, "Help me? You are the nurse, aren't you?" Yes, let me teach you how to better care for yourself. Patients can be extremely sick and still live.

After beginning work as a nurse, it was exciting. But there is also a degree of hesitancy. I am now the one who was tasked with assessing my patients and calling the doctors. After working as a nurse for six months, I was told I would be the charge nurse. "Why me?" The reply was comical, but serious. "There is no one else." My charge nurse called and spoke with me. "You have supported me so much, this you can do, I have no doubt." It went well. New nurse. New facility. New doctors. We all had to get to know one another. Once they realized I knew what I was doing, they slowed down with the nonsense questions. Granted, I was relief charge nurse; later after a year, I became advisor which meant I was delegated to orient the new nurses. I enjoyed that part. Sharing my knowledge and the policies with them. Who knew a few years ago this could be possible? I emphasized teamwork. Holding them up to support them and pushing them to be their best.

My career has been fulfilling; this has been the best career

I could NOT have chosen. More doors have opened for me, all because of this career. Great opportunities I never knew existed have been presented to me. I can truly say I am enjoying the journey. Sharing experiences and portions of my testimony regarding challenges with students when they feel like giving up has provided them the best example that is relatable. I have been an instructor and mentor. It is gratifying to see them from student to nurse.

Once God gave me a glance back over my career, He showed me from beginning to present. I know it was God who brought me through and sustained me. It is what He has best for me. The hurts, the disappointments. Listen to your heart, do not ignore that unction. God is speaking to you.

ABOUT THE AUTHOR

Carolyn Pickens Coleman is a daughter, wife, mother, sister, cousin, friend, and co-worker from Bessemer, Alabama. She has a B.S. in Nursing from Samford University and an M.A. in Health Service Administration from Strayer University. Carolyn is a member of the Birmingham Black Nurses Association, Inc., serving as the Chairperson of the Outreach committee, and is the current President of the Bessemer Public Library Trustee Board. She has a big heart and volunteers in her community.

Carolyn has more than 36 years of experience as a critical care nurse and spent five years as a nurse case manager. She worked with hospital administrators to establish plans regarding complex patient cases, concentrating on outcome management, utilizing best practices, advocating for patients. She is also an adjunct instructor.

Carolyn is the author of four books a series about Gentry who faces her life choices, as we all do, *Happiness Hurt Healing, The Re-Entry of Gentry, Gentry's Journey,* and *Gentry's Circle of Friends.* For Carolyn, writing is cathartic. She enjoys reading and staying active by line dancing, walking, and spending time with her family and friends.

Carolyn joins a group of esteemed authors in *The Breaking Point* and hopes that her chapter will give you the insight to find your passion and purpose for a meaningful life.

Connect with Carolyn

- Email: cpwcoleman@gmail.com.

19

RESTORED

Lisa Marie Morton

I'm trying to keep my composure, but tears of disappointment and excruciating pain are rolling down my face and gently landing onto my children's clothes I'm folding in the laundry room. I can hear the clanging of hangers while the clothes are being taken off of them. My husband is upstairs packing to leave me. Earlier he set me down and said, " Lisa, I want a divorce! I've always cheated on you, and I just want out. I'm leaving today."

I stood there in the laundry room as I watched my husband walk out the front door. I instantly collapsed on the floor in heartbreaking agony. The shirt I was folding was drenched with tears—I wept by the dryer as my high school sweetheart—the man I've been with since I was fourteen years old—was driving off to be with another woman. After all of the infidelity, emotional abuse, and physical abuse I endured in our toxic relationship, I probably should've been happy he left. But, instead I was devastated. I loved my husband. I convinced myself for so long a miracle would take place in my marriage. Instead, I watched the foundation I built crumble. My life was completely out of my control. As I lay there in pain, I thought to myself who will ever love me? Suicidal thoughts flooded my mind. As I got deeper into the fantasy of taking my life, I heard a still small voice push its way through the dark thoughts that consumed my mind and say, "I will never leave you nor forsake you!" I said, "God, the pain is just too much to bear, I feel like I could just die!" Suddenly, the darkness lifted and I felt God. Love and peace completely engulfed me. Then I heard, "And God shall wipe away all tears from their eyes; and there shall be no more death, neither sorrow, nor crying, neither shall there be any more pain: for the former things are passed away" (Revelation 21:4 KJV). God said "I will resurrect your marriage into a better union." You will see a miracle! Will you Trust me?

I wanted to be able to say yes, but I doubted. I loved my husband, but I just didn't see how he could ever be the husband and father we needed him to be. I then heard God say, " Let him go! Release him for the former things have passed away. Lean on me! Will you partner with me?" In tears, I said, "Yes!" It was in the laundry room at this very moment that I reached my breaking point. I made the decision to stop doing life my way and partner

with God and do life His way. My submission and obedience caused me to have a relationship with God like
never before. I began to know Him personally. The journey to restoration was difficult, yet beautiful, because
God was by my side. At times I felt like my life was being
turned upside down, but in fact my life was slowly being
turned right side up. The materialistic, sad, lost, oblivious, and confused woman I was before was dying and a
woman after God's heart was emerging from the ashes.
As I look back, I realize the significance of my breakthrough taking place in the laundry room. The laundry
room is a place of storage as well as washing and renewal.
God completely exposed the issues I stored away for so
long. The dirty laundry of my life was everywhere, and it
was time for me to undertake it and get it in order. Being
in the middle of a mess, you didn't want to attend to
could be overwhelming, but not when God is with you in
it. The Bible says in Psalm 139:8 (KJV) "If I ascend up into
heaven, thou art there: if I make my bed in hell, behold,
thou art there." Meaning God is with us through it all.
God loves us too much to leave us in a mess. I built a life
that looked good to others, but in reality it was a facade.
God has a way of putting a stop to counterfeit living. God
didn't want me to settle for what looked good, I needed to
strive for what was authentically good. After I completely
yielded to God, God began to introduce me to myself.
The me who needed repentance and healing and the me
I was to become. I had to acknowledge all of my faults in

my marriage. I'd spent so long blaming my husband for our problems that I didn't acknowledge I was also a problem. One day in prayer, God revealed my heart to me as well as my husband's heart. My heart was unforgiving and cold, and my husband's heart was hurt, lost, and seeking to be loved.

Throughout our marriage, I'd allowed my heart to turn cold toward my husband which negatively influenced how I treated him. God asked me to forgive my husband. I released my husband from all the pain he caused me and forgave him at that moment. Immediately I felt liberated . A huge weight was lifted off of me.

God then told me I needed to war for my marriage. I said, "God, but the divorce papers are finalized. It's over!" God said, "Old things die. I am doing a new thing!" God brought me into another level of praying that was new for me. He said, "Your husband hurt you because he is a broken person. It will be your love and prayers that lead him into repentance, healing, and wholeness." I aligned with God and began praying for my husband. I learned to battle the devil who was my true enemy. A couple of weeks later, God said, "Now I need you to show me your faith. Go clean out the other master closet and make space for your husband's return." I said, "But he lives with another woman. They're talking about marriage and children."

God said, "I will send the other woman far away never to be a problem for you. Do you trust me?"

I submitted myself unto God, I put my faith to work, and emptied out the second master closet, fully believing God's Word. I chose to believe what God spoke to me in spite of my current situation. I began to live with expectancy. About a month later, the loss of a beloved family member brought us together as we traveled to my hometown. After a few days together, he said he would like us to reconcile. I asked about his girlfriend. He said they broke up, and she moved across the country. I thought to myself, Wow! God did it. He then began to tell me he wanted us to attend counseling and reconcile correctly. He said, "I never want to hurt you again, You deserve a good man." Our first step towards restoration was acknowledging what went wrong and making the decision to fix the issues. We attended counseling individually and as a couple. On the road to restoration, we cut toxic people out of our lives and downsized our business. We shifted our focus where it belonged, which was on our marriage and children. The adjustment wasn't easy, but it was essential to the success of our family. God gave us better than we lost. We remarried on March 5th representing the Bible verse (Proverbs 3:5 KJV) "Trust in the Lord with all thine heart; and lean not unto thine own understanding." Restoration wouldn't have been possible if we leaned on our own understanding, we needed to trust God in the process. We then had our marriage ceremony on the beach July 25th representing the Bible verse Matthew 7:25 (KJV). "And the rain descended, and the floods came, and the winds blew, and beat upon that house; and it fell not: for it was founded upon a rock." This verse represents God now being the center of our marriage. No storm will tear us down because we are firmly built on Jesus. People always ask: Why did you have to get fully divorced? The answer is simple. Our marriage had to fully die before God could resurrect a new one.

I can honestly say the problems our marriage once suffered we suffer no more! All things are new because I trusted God, and we followed these five God-inspired steps.

Give your situation to God, and make Jesus the center of your life individually and as a couple.

Old problems and habits must die (never bring up the past, MOVE ON!); repentance and a renewal of mind is key.

Healing and forgiveness (counseling)

Set boundaries and goals for your marriage and give it to each other (communication).

Both of you must focus on the solution and always work

towards the goals set for your marriage which should include to love, honor, and respect one another always and forever forsaking all others!

ABOUT THE AUTHOR

Lisa Marie Morton is a co-author in the book *The Breaking Point*. An entrepreneur, wife, coach, evangelist, and magazine publisher, she masterfully balances ministry, career, and family. She has ministered throughout the U.S., bringing a powerful message of unshakable faith.

Due to her impactful testimony, she carries a deep passion when it comes to teaching on the importance of having an intimate relationship with Jesus Christ and partnering with Him in forgiveness, self deliverance, and soul healing.

She is committed to equipping the body of Christ to go into the camp of the enemy and take back everything he stole from them, as well as raising leaders to radiate light and take their place in the world being pillars in their fam-

166

ilies and communities while pushing back the darkness by adopting the principles of Jesus Christ.

She is also the founder of Let There Be Light Worldwide Ministries which offers free counseling through licensed professional counselors and therapists. Mental health, family restoration, and personal development is their mission. She is also the visionary behind the From The Pit To The Palace conference which inspires people to get out of the pits of life and use it for their good.

Lisa Marie lives in Orlando, Florida with her husband who is also her high school sweetheart and their three beautiful children. She enjoys spending time with her family, taking family vacations, snowboarding, fashion, and cooking.

Connect with Lisa

- www.lisamariemorton.com
- www.Belightworldwide.com

20

GRIEF

Dr. Harriet Roberson

Growing up as an Army Brat and a PK (Preachers Kid) in a large family of ten, I had a relatively good life. We were not rich but lacked little. We travelled and lived all over the United States and in several States in Germany. I went from my parent's home to commuter in college, to my husband's home, so I always had family close by. Once married, we had kids right away and settled into a beautiful family life. Thanksgiving was the annual family get together. It was always such a happy time enjoying our parents, the eight kids and lots of grandchildren. Our mother was an extremely great cook, so the food was amazing and plentiful. Although it was mostly fun, we had the occasional family fight between the siblings but always made up before leaving town to go to our respective homes all over the country.

We thought this would be our life adding more grandkids

and great grandkids and our parents would grow old together like we saw on television.

Somewhere along the way LIFE happened! I had so many family deaths in a brief period. In less than six years, my oldest brother was tragically murdered, my mother died so young at sixty years old, my dad remarried shortly after our mother's death. He married a woman who caused even more grief/pain as she tried to keep us from our father. My baby sister committed suicide, my dad passed a few years later. My other brother who I was the closest to died after a lengthy illness, my mother-in-law passed, and my son-in-law's father passed suddenly at age fifty-five years.

So much pain/grief, such wonderful people. Christians! I asked God, "WHY"?

All the nasty mean people in the world and you take such good people? As I heard a preacher say, "Lord, why do you keep taking my good members, I have some others that you can take now." It sounds bad that believers could feel like that, but I am being transparent about what drove me to my breaking point.

I was so angry about my mother's death. My mom dedicated her life to God and the ministry. She took over the church responsibilities when my father became extremely ill from cancer. She waited on him hand and foot, she preached, teached, played the piano for services and even cleaned bathrooms in the church as needed. I was so mad because I felt like this is how she is repaid for her hard work and dedication? Yes, as a believer I questioned God. And guess what; He did not answer.

I felt betrayed by God. As though what was the purpose of dedicating my life to Him and the church only to watch others who sacrificed, tragically die? I became extremely angry and very bitter! I was mad, annoyed, and impatient all the time. Mad at my husband, the drivers in traffic, the people in stores, even the "blessed/highly favored" people at church. And the poor referees at my kid's sports. Yes, I was that obnoxious mom! I wanted nothing to do with the church or with God.

I started to isolate and did not want to be around people. Most nights I was on the couch with snacks and wine coolers watching soap operas. I gained weight which made me feel unattractive. It became easier to stay home than to let people see me at the lowest point in my life. I mean, what would "they" think if "they" saw me looking crazy.

One day my daughter asked, "Mom, why are you so sad"? My son asked, "Why do I have a nice Mommy and a Mean Mommy"?

Seriously, that was my breaking point. I felt as though I

stay angry with husband, but my kids were everything to me and they deserved more.

I sought God's guidance on how to work through this grief. I first had to admit I needed more help than the "pray for me" post on Facebook. I had to get off the couch, turn off the soaps and get myself together.

I looked online and found a Christian Grief Counselor, and it changed my life. *I learned* how to process my emotions. I developed strategies and methods for coping with my losses and the grief that was bringing me down so far to the feeling of anger and hopelessness.

I started praying for myself. I became grateful for those who are presently in my life. I even started thanking God for the time He allowed the person to be in my life and what I learned from them. When I got sad, I started thinking of funny things the person did and it put a smile on my face.

I started searching for scriptures on grief, then studied and meditated on them. These are a few that made the most impact.

Psalm 73:26 (KJV) "My flesh and my heart faileth: *but* God *is* the strength of my heart, and my portion for ever." Matthew 5:4 (KJV) "Blessed *are* they that mourn: for they shall be comforted." Although my mom had cancer, she died from a blood clot that was a result from the exploratory surgery to do a biopsy on a tumor. I know my mom would not have wanted people poking and prodding over her, nor losing her hair. I know my brother was tired of fighting and taking ten pills a day. He fought long enough to attend his youngest child's high school graduation. My father was tired, he suffered several strokes that took his speech and his eyesight. He could not walk on his own, had to be helped to the bathroom and cleaned up by others and be spoon fed. What type of quality of life is that to have? We are the selfish ones, wanting to keep our loved ones here for us and not for them.

I learned to take comfort in knowing that although we miss our loved ones, they are in a better place, with no pain and suffering. And they are getting the reward that we are striving to get to. Living to live again in Heaven

I found comforting scriptures such as.

John 16:33 (KJV) "These things I have spoken unto you, that in me ye might have peace. In the world ye shall have tribulation: but be of good cheer; I have overcome the world."

Philippians 4:7 (KJV) "And the peace of God, which passeth all understanding, shall keep your hearts and minds through Christ Jesus."

I learned being a Christian does not mean we are exempt from trials and tribulations, including death of loved ones.

I learned that when I trust God and not lean to my own understanding, He will give me peace that I do not have on my own. A peace that comes from heaven to wrap His arms around me and give me a sweet sleep.

I also had to come to the realization that although I am sad, my kids are sad too. They have lost a special person in their life as well. And it is my responsibility to let them know it is okay and very appropriate to grieve and to cry, especially our boys and men. I reminded them and even encouraged myself to know in our hearts, how much they loved us. We must not only live a life to make them proud, but we must live this life right so we will see them again.

Grief counseling is necessary for kids who do not understand death and why Grandma or Grandpa is no longer coming to visit me or me visit them. Grief counseling is highly recommended for most people to fully live again when a loved one close to them dies.

I learned that no loss is too small to ask for support. I recently suggested to a friend who lost their pet to seek help from a counselor. I also recommended grief counseling to a friend who lost several members of their family within a month's time. They were having what is commonly called "Survivor's Guilt." They were feeling guilt for moving on without their family that was no longer with them.

I learned that grief counseling will guide *you* to talk about the loss and what the person meant to you. Also, counselors give you a safe place to talk about the circumstances surrounding a *death. Especially when a murder or suicide is involved.*

Through it all, I learned these things; God is bigger than death. He can make you sing and dance even amid your deepest pain. I learned that although we do not understand many things that happen to us, especially death, we must accept what God allows.

And as far as the "they" I was worried about seeing me at my lowest, at my breaking point, I had to ask myself, who is the "they" anyway?

ABOUT THE AUTHOR

Dr. Harriet Roberson is co-author of *The Breaking Point.*

TV personality/host, motivational/inspirational speaker, networking strategist, professional recruiter/headhunter. author, entrepreneur, and philanthropist. Dr. Harriet is the President of Learning and Development as well as a speaker trainer with National Association of Minority Speakers and serves on several boards.

Dr. Harriet is known as the Kingdom Connector, Harriet is the co-founder of WEN (Women's Empowerment Network), Great Marriages Rock and ImpactHer Women's Fellowship.

Dr. Harriet is married to her husband of forty years and together they have two married daughters, a son and two grandsons.

Connect with Dr. Harriet

- www.HarrietRoberson.com
- FB/Twitter/IG: @harrietroberson

Book Reviews

Did you enjoy *The Breaking Point*?

Please consider writing a book review on Amazon and Barnes & Noble.

Book reviews are important to authors and it only takes a few minutes to write one.

A review doesn't have to be long. A few short sentences or a few words to describe the book works just fine.

Book Recommendations

Since you've enjoyed reading *The Breaking Point* will you help me promote it?

Here's how you can help.

- Kindly recommend it to books clubs and other readers.
- Ask your library to carry a copy.
- Order another copy to give away instead of passing The Breaking Point around.

- Share it on social media as a book recommendation.
- Invite us to discuss the book either by Clubhouse, Facebook Live or a visit to your city.

Visionary Author Paulette Harper

www.pauletteharper.com

Thank you so much!!

Made in USA - Kendallville, IN
71425_9781737093145
04.29.2022 1517